T0032525

HOW TO GET OVER A BREAKUP

ANCIENT WISDOM FOR MODERN READERS

■ ■ ■ ■

For a full list of titles in the series, go to https://press.princeton.edu
/series/ancient-wisdom-for-modern-readers.

HOW TO GET OVER A BREAKUP

An Ancient Guide to Moving On

Ovid

Translated and introduced
by Michael Fontaine

PRINCETON UNIVERSITY PRESS

PRINCETON & OXFORD

Published by Princeton University Press
41 William Street, Princeton, New Jersey 08540
99 Banbury Road, Oxford OX2 6JX

press.princeton.edu

ISBN 9780691220307
ISBN (e-book) 9780691220314

British Library Cataloging-in-Publication Data is available

Editorial: Rob Tempio and Chloe Coy
Production Editorial: Natalie Baan
Text Design: Pamela L. Schnitter
Jacket Design: Heather Hansen
Production: Erin Suydam
Publicity: Tyler Hubbert and Carmen Jimenez

Jacket image: *Cupid and Psyche standing*.
Courtesy of Louvre Museum, Department of Sculptures
of the Middle Ages, Renaissance, and Modern Times

This book has been composed in Stempel Garamond LT Std

Printed in the United States of America

1 3 5 7 9 10 8 6 4 2

A morior! Dum quod amem cogor,
   et non amor.
I will die of despair—forced into passions no
   partner will share!
—*CARMINA BURANA* (116),
   TR. DAVID PARLETT

Me miseram, quod amor non est medicabilis
   herbis!
Ah, what a plight! Because love isn't something
   that medicine fixes.
—OVID, *HEROIDES* 5.149

CONTENTS

INTRODUCTION

Breaking up is horrible. It is world-ending. All kinds of relationships come to an end or change, and futures we had dreamed of will never happen. Breakups can play games with our minds and bring on overwhelming feelings of grief. And practical problems ensue, too. Sometimes we need all new friends, or a new place to live. No wonder, then, that breakups are so often compared to "losing a loved one"; the expression itself evokes the analogy with death.

This is not just a subjective impression. In 1967, a pair of psychiatrists sought to quantify and rank the most stressful events in life. The result is the famous Holmes and Rahe Stress Scale. In first place comes the death of a spouse. Tied for fourth are going to prison and the death of a close family member. Then come personal injury or illness, marriage, and getting fired.[1] These are events so stressful, psychologists say, they can make us physically sick—and desperate for help. So, what's in second and third place?

You guessed it. Divorce and marital separation.

With stakes like these, can anyone—much less a poet from ancient Rome two thousand years ago—really help us through it all?

That may sound absurd. Psychotherapy is surely not the first image that *Greece* or *Rome* brings to mind. The Colosseum, maybe, or the Parthenon or the *Iliad*. But a clinical psychologist?

If that's jarring, then consider the case of Antiphon. A contemporary of the philosopher Socrates, Antiphon of Rhamnus (480–411 BCE) eventually became an influential statesman in classical Athens. His first career, however, had been different:

Antiphon devised an art of relieving distress, as physicians treat people who are sick. In Corinth, he set up shop in a small building near the market square and advertised his ability to treat people in distress with talk therapy (*dia logōn therapeuein*). After learning the causes, he would talk patients out of feeling bad. [. . .] He also announced a series of "antidepressant lectures," which would show how no heartache was so great that he couldn't banish it from the mind.

The clinic, the clinician, the clientele, the claims, the cures: here is psychoanalysis in all but name, twenty-four hundred years before Sigmund Freud set up shop in Vienna. And sure enough, in a book titled *Getting Along*, Antiphon offered advice on dealing with setbacks, money, boredom, unrealistic hopes, self-control, and marriage. It's no surprise, then, that he also allegedly wrote a book on *The Interpretation of Dreams*.[2]

The poem translated here as *How to Get Over a Breakup* suggests that two thousand years ago, practitioners like Antiphon and Freud were plying their trade under the archways of ancient Rome. As we shall see, Ovid, our poet, poses as a relationship counselor no different from his counterparts today, citing case histories and dispensing lightly medicalized advice to help cure us of unrequited love.

And what Ovid has to say won't just surprise and entertain you. It can help you, too.

> *Quot caelum stellas, tot habet tua Roma puellas.*
> Stars up above are outnumbered by girls here in Rome who could use love!
> —OVID, *THE ART OF LOVE* (1.59)

Publius Ovidius Naso was born more than four centuries after Antiphon, in 43 BCE. He died in 17 CE, leaving behind the world's first autobiography.[3] Best known for writing *Metamorphoses* (*Changes of Shape*), one of the most well-known surviving works of Roman literature, Ovid was also Rome's most perceptive—and irreverent—psychologist. *Metamorphoses* is a massive retelling of mythological stories in classical epic form. Most stories end with a character transforming into a new shape or state or being, with sexual attraction or repulsion typically serving as the catalyst of such changes. And in narrating each story, Ovid explores the psychology of love in many sensitive, subtle, and unexpected ways.

Born ninety miles outside the city, Ovid moved to Rome for his schooling and fell in love with it. From then on, Rome and love became central to his worldview. He could have told you that *amor*, love, is *Roma* spelled backwards—and did you see *amor* hiding in the Greek title *Metamorphoses*?

For Ovid, Rome was *the* city of romance. Romeos were everywhere, and so were Rome-grown beauties. He'd insisted on that point in an important prequel to *How to Get Over a Breakup*. Titled *Ars Amatoria*—in English, *The Art of Love*—that prequel is a poem in three books. The first two books were intended to teach the men of Rome how to find and keep a girlfriend, while the third offers women strategies for finding a man. Posing as a "professor of love," Ovid was semiseriously teaching his readers techniques and rules for seducing the opposite sex.

(Yes, the opposite sex. Ovid writes about several queer and nonbinary relationships in *Metamorphoses*, but in his love poetry proper he only talks about women and men. Still, his advice undoubtedly applies more broadly.)

In the middle of the year 1 CE, Ovid published the sequel translated here.[4] Titled *Remedia Amoris*—literally, *Remedies for Love*—the poem completes his systematic "treatise" on love, and it brings us full circle: from no relationship, to relationship, to no relationship. Even better, this time he addresses his book to women and men alike.

(Or so he says, anyway. As we'll soon see, some of his advice doesn't seem applicable to men and women alike. It's a recurring problem, and it won't take long to notice. More on that in a moment.)

Ars Amatoria is about falling in love; *Remedia Amoris* is about climbing back out of it. But that symmetry masks an important change of perspective. In *Ars Amatoria*, love is desirable and good. In *Remedia Amoris*, love is a force of ill—indeed, of illness itself. This time, love is lovesickness. It is an emotional wound that requires an antidote, like a snakebite, or a disease that requires medical treatment. Over and over Ovid characterizes love as a physical or psychological injury—a *vitium* (blemish), a *morbus* (illness), a *vulnus* (wound). Accordingly, he prescribes thirty-eight practical suggestions and coping strategies for dealing with a broken heart or a breakup. At times, he even speaks in the voice of a former addict himself, much like a substance-abuse counselor who goes into that line of work because he has benefitted from counseling in his own life.

Yet once again, because the text is frequently humorous, hilarious even, it's never clear how serious Ovid is. The problem is that Ovid is a gleeful provocateur. He is the kind of man who tries to talk you into increasingly crazy ideas, seeing how far he can push it, until you finally protest and he announces, with a grin, "Just kidding!"

In practice, this means Ovid's intentions are never clear. He offers a great variety of tricks and tactics and cures to get over love. Some are insightful and valuable, while others strain credulity; they're presumably effective, but unsavory or immoral or just plain evil. It may well be that Ovid is taking a "whatever works" approach and genuinely means what he says. As he says himself of his recommendations,

> Someone might say that that's silly ("they're small!")—which is, in fact, true—but things that are useless themselves, little by little add up.... So, just be sure to seek safety in numbers. Compile all my rules, and integrate them: out of steps, far-reaching systems emerge.

Or maybe he's just kidding, and the joke's really on us.

> *Omnis amans amens.*
> Every romantic is frantic.
> —LATIN PROVERB

The idea that love is like an illness has been around a long time, and there's obviously something to it: the infatuation, the fantasizing, the pounding pulse, the sweaty palms, the flush; and conversely—when love isn't reciprocated—the heartache, the sleeplessness, the prayers, the anguish, the grief. We've all felt it. This is why Greeks before Ovid connected the goddess Aphrodite with *aphrosyne* (stupidity) and the god Eros with *eris* (quarreling), and why Romans saw connections between *cupidus* (longing) and *stupidus* (gaga), between *amare* (loving) and *amarum* (distressing, hard to take), and between *amor* (love) and *mors* (death).

Nevertheless, Ovid's idea of "treating" or "curing" love was something striking and original and new, and the way he developed it is ingenious. In *Remedies for Love*, he does not simply reverse all his prescriptions in his book on love. Ovid knew that love doesn't work that way. *Not* hitting on someone you're attracted to doesn't produce the opposite effect of hitting on him or her. *Not* kissing or holding hands with someone you love doesn't produce the opposite feelings that kissing or holding hands with someone you love will. Where, then, did he get his ideas on coping with or curing love? And how seriously did he mean them?

One answer is that he found them in Hellenistic philosophy. Just as there are several major "schools" of psychotherapy in competition today—Freudian, Jungian, client-centered, and so forth—so there were several major "schools" or denominations of philosophy in competition in ancient Rome. The Stoics, the Epicureans, the Peripatetics—all offered their adherents books and therapeutic strategies for dealing with woe. About forty-five years before Ovid wrote *Remedies for Love*, the Roman statesman Cicero alluded to them in the *Tusculan Disputations*. This book was his own guide to mental health, and it consolidated Stoic and other ideas. "There are established terms that are often used," remarks Cicero,

> with regard to poverty, and certain words that are used when describing a life deficient in public honors or glory. There are

separate and specific treatises relating to the topics of exile, destruction of one's country, servitude, physical debility, blindness, and on every event we may call a calamity. These topics the Greeks separate into different books. . . . For each of these situations, there is a distinct and suitable consolation.[5]

These are the kind of self-help books of which Ovid's poem is both parody and part. We know this because Ovid lifted several recommendations directly from a later portion of the *Tusculan Disputations*, a portion in which Cicero discusses lust and love:

The necessary cure (*curatio*) for someone affected by this [love or lust] is to show him how unimportant, worthless, and completely inconsequential is the thing he ardently desires, how easily it can either be obtained somewhere else or through a different method, or how it can be completely disregarded. Sometimes his attention should be directed to other studies, worries, cares (*curas*), and activities. The sick who are not recuperating are often cured (*curandus*) by a change of physical residence. Some also think that the memory of an old love can be dispelled by a new one, as one nail forces out another.[6]

It is from this very passage that Ovid's recommendations in lines 143–44, 151–52, and 214 come. (Some stranger borrowings from Cicero's contemporary, Lucretius, will be pointed out in the translation when we come to them.)

Despite that debt to Cicero, however, here is where things start to get interesting. Cicero goes on to state an opinion that Ovid read and then rejected:

But above all he [a person affected by love] must be instructed on how powerful love's unchecked fury can be. Of all the perturbations of the mind, there is certainly none more vehement. And even if you do not want to denounce love—and here I am talking about the excesses of illicit sex, enticement, adultery, and finally incest, all of which have an ugliness that deserves to be denounced—the mind's distress in the throes of love is horrible in itself, even if you *leave out* these excesses.

Ovid disagrees. His coping strategies do *not* denounce or demonize love—in fact, Ovid explicitly declines to do so in the charming allegory with which his poem begins.

This is the point to grasp clearly and not lose sight of. Ovid *believes* in love. He is optimistic about it. When it goes bad, he keeps it personal and specific. He does not recommend swearing off relationships, or commitment, or women, or men, or other people entirely. No men going their own way, no women quitting on men, no revenge promiscuity, no revenge celibacy. The temptation is obviously there. It's implied by Cicero. Yet Ovid edits it right out. Shake off the dust and try again, he says.

For Ovid, breakups and divorces and unrequited love are painful, yes, but normal, natural, and they should simply bring us back to the starting point to try again with someone else.

> The path of progress in psychiatry is circular,
> periodically returning to its starting point.
> —THOMAS SZASZ, *THE MANUFACTURE OF*
> *MADNESS* (1970)

Throughout antiquity, and as late as the fourth century CE, lovesickness was seen as a metaphorical illness. Physicians regarded it as a psychological problem, and they prescribed feel-good remedies like Ovid's. Lovesick patients, recommended Galen (129–216)—who was a philosopher as well as a doctor—ought "to take frequent baths, to drink wine, to ride, and to see and hear everything pleasurable."[7]

With the fall of Rome in the West, something changed. By the year 1100, as science began to recover in Italy, lovesickness had been reinterpreted as an actual illness—specifically, a brain disease. "Love, which is also called eros," declared Constantine the African, the most influential medical writer of the time (died c. 1087), "is a disease touching the brain."[8] The evidence had not changed, and lovesickness had not been cured out of existence. Yet the idea caught on.

In 1496, Battista Fregoso (1450–1505), a former doge of Genoa, added political clout to psychiatric belief in declaring that "love is not only like an illness, it is an actual illness—and dangerous."[9] Remedies for love became increasingly medicalized and, in some cases, pharmacological: that is, pills and drugs.

In the twenty-first century this view is gradually going away, and therapists are increasingly turning to Cognitive Behavioral Therapy (CBT) to heal broken hearts. CBT is talk therapy. In CBT sessions, the therapist helps a patient learn to recognize and reevaluate patterns of negative thinking and hence manage stress more easily. CBT emphasizes the distinction between things we cannot control, like situations, and things we can, like our judgment about or reaction to those situations. Many find CBT highly effective for breakups. Innovative as it may sound, however, CBT is merely ancient Stoicism under a new name.[10] And since Stoic talk therapy was a major source of Ovid's recommendations in the first place, it seems we're closing the circle.

With the onset of social media, moreover, Ovid's advice has become relevant in a new way. Two thousand years ago, Ovid was writing for an audience based in the city of Rome. His readers couldn't just up and leave town if a relationship went bad. They had to find a way to move on, while realizing they'd probably run into their ex again.

It's the same in our hyperconnected world today. Twenty years ago, you *could* still up and leave town. Not anymore. You may unfriend your ex, but the algorithm ensures you'll see reminders—and friends of "friends"—for a long time to come.

For anyone who finds our new reality painful, Ovid may have something to tell us yet.

A Note on the Translation

Ovid's text is a poem in elegiac couplets, a traditional Greek meter widely used in Latin. In this meter, as you can see on the printed page, the odd-numbered lines are longer. They are six-beat "dactylic hexameters," consisting of long and short syllables in various combinations. The even-numbered lines are shorter. They also have six beats and they begin exactly like the odd lines. Unlike the odd lines, though, they then split directly in half, pause, and begin again. Verses 41–42, which imitate a carnival barker's patter, are a nice illustration of how this works:

> *Ád mea, déceptí iuvenés, praecépta veníte,*
> **quós** *suus* **éx** *omní* (pause here) **párte** *feféllit*
> *amór.*

> **Stép** right **úp**, all you **ná**ïve **víc**tims! *Cóme* to
> my **díc**tums
> —*íf* you're a **foól** for **love** (pause here), *ór* been
> bam**boóz**led, be**trá**yed!

In the even lines, you'll occasionally find a rhyme at the end of each half. When you do, the rhyming words are typically a noun and adjective in agreement.

INTRODUCTION

Why translate Ovid—who wrote in verse—
as prose, as I've chosen? Simple: nobody reads
poetry much anymore. Still, though, I've aped
the original rhythm throughout the translation.
Read it aloud, and you'll hear cadences striking
your ear.

A QUICK START GUIDE
TO *REMEDIES FOR LOVE*

> *Expedit esse deos, et, ut expedit, esse putemus.*
> Having the gods exist pays off; since it pays,
>   let's believe it.
> —OVID, *THE ART OF LOVE* (1.637)

Ovid was an atheist (that line above became immensely popular in the Enlightenment). In his poetry, though, he affects to converse with gods, and he exploits popular myths about them constantly. The following are the three most important gods here:

- **Cupid,** who has two names in Latin: *Cupído* (meaning *Desire*) and *Amor* (meaning *Love*). His Greek name, Eros, gives us the word *erotic.* Cupid is imagined as an angel with wings—either a cherub or a young man— holding torches. He wields a bow with which he fires off the arrows (*tela*) that fire up love.

- **Venus** (meaning *Sex*) is Cupid's mother. Her name yields *venom* (from *venenum*, a love potion) and, yes, *venereal*. Her Greek name, Aphrodite, gives us *aphrodisiac*. She is married to Vulcan (god of volcanos) but consorts with Mars (god of warfare and "martial" arts). In Homer's *Iliad*, she fights in the war, but is wounded by the hero Diomedes.
- **Apollo** is the god of both poetry and healing, and hence, for this therapeutic poem, doubly relevant. He wears a crown of laurel in his hair, carries a lyre, and, like Cupid, wields a bow and arrow.

Like all Roman philosophers, Ovid argues from anecdotes. He takes many illustrative examples from mythology and legendary history, especially stories connected with the Trojan War (1194–1184 BCE). Like many teachers, he expects you to either know the stories or go look them up. He takes a special interest here in Phyllis, whose story he tells in lines 591–608,

and Circe (263–90). Circe, the enticing enchant-
ress of Homer's *Odyssey*, dwelled on a promontory just south of Rome named Monte Circeo.
Against all the odds, Ulysses (Odysseus), king
of Ithaca, summoned the strength to leave her.
Other allusions are explained in the endnotes.

Finally, Ovid is a shock artist, and one of his
techniques here is to shock the "patient" back
to reality. When he uses coarse or demeaning
language, therefore, so do I. For example, Ovid
routinely calls women "girls" (*puellae*), and in
one case he refers to "humping" (*inire*). And
worse. Given the explicit defense he makes of
his art halfway through the poem (see appendix 2), it would be a mistake to pretend he does
not say these things. Attempts to censor Ovid
began in his own lifetime and have never stopped.
Bucking that trend, this edition opts instead to
indicate where Ovid seems determined to cause
offense, and to suggest reasons why.

P. Ovidi Nasonis

REMEDIA AMORIS

REMEDIES FOR LOVE

By Publius Ovidius Naso

LEGERAT HUIUS AMOR titulum nomenque libelli:
    "Bella mihi, video, bella parantur" ait.

"¡Parce tuum vatem sceleris damnare, Cupido,
    tradita qui toties te duce signa tuli!
Non ego Tydides, a quo tua saucia mater   5
    in liquidum rediit aethera Martis equis.
Saepe tepent alii iuvenes; ego semper amavi,
    et si, quid faciam, nunc quoque, quaeris, amo.

PRELUDE

A Close Call

LOVE GOT A PEEK at the title and name that I'd picked for this guidebook. "War!" He gasped, "so I see! Plans for a war . . . against *me*!"

The Poet Defends Himself

"Perish the thought! Cupid, don't accuse me— Your *apostle!*—of sinning. Don't forget, I'm the one who carried the banner for You. I'm not some Diomedes, who wounded Your mother and sent Her clear to the sky in retreat, borrowing horses from Mars. Typically, other young men lose heat, but I'm always a lover. (Even right now, if you ask—yes, I'm ready for love.)

Quin etiam docui qua possis arte parari,
 et quod nunc ratio est, impetus ante fuit. 10
Nec te, blande puer, nec nostras prodimus artes,
 nec nova praeteritum Musa retexit opus.
Siquis amat quod amare iuvat, feliciter ardens
 gaudeat, et vento naviget ille suo;

at siquis male fert indignae regna puellae, 15
 ne pereat, nostrae sentiat artis opem.

¿Cur aliquis laqueo collum nodatus amator
 a trabe sublimi triste pependit onus?
¿Cur aliquis rigido fodit sua pectora ferro?
 Invidiam caedis, pacis amator, habes. 20

Qui, nisi desierit, misero periturus amore est,
 desinat; et nulli funeris auctor eris.
Et puer es, nec te quicquam nisi ludere oportet:

Let's get real: I even taught a whole *method* to get You! Once it was all hit-or-miss; now it's turned into an art. I'm no traitor to You, little cherub, or to my own system; this new poem doesn't undo all of that previous work. Someone's in love? And likes what he loves? Terrific! Keep going! It's smooth sailing for him. (Have a great time, lucky guy!)

If, though, a man's chafing under the yoke, if his girlfriend's a tyrant, there's no need to die! Show him this book—it'll help:

Why have some men in love turned a lasso
    into a necktie? And, sad sacks that they
    are, hung themselves from a high beam?
Why have some men in love stabbed them-
    selves in the chest with a knife thrust?

Well, Mr. 'I-Promote-Peace,' *You're* getting blamed for their deaths![11]

Somebody can't quit love? He'll literally *die* of it? Let him quit: Fine! You're off the hook— guilty of nobody's death. You're just a kid; Your only job is to play and be happy. Play, then!

lude; decent annos mollia regna tuos.   24
Vitricus et gladiis et acuta dimicet hasta,   27
   et victor multa caede cruentus eat;
tu cole maternas, tutò quibus utimur, artes,
   et quarum vitio nulla fit orba parens.   30

Effice nocturna frangatur ianua rixa,
   et tegat ornatas multa corona fores;
fac coeant furtim iuvenes timidaeque puellae,
   verbaque dent cauto qualibet arte viro;
et modo blanditias rigido, modo iurgia, posti   35
   dicat et exclusus flebile cantet amans.
His lacrimis contentus eris sine crimine mortis;
   non tua fax avidos digna subire rogos."

Simple concerns suit You at this stage of life. Let
Your stepfather, Mars, brandish weapons—the
swords and the sharp spears. He can go deci-
mate foes, triumph, all covered in blood; You
ought to practice Your *mother's* arts. We can
handle those safely, and there's no risk of mis-
fire leaving a parent bereft:

> Rival suitors should bust down the door
>   when they brawl, serenading! Make
>   them! And make their festoons curtain
>   the jambs of the door![12]
> Help a young man and his nervous girl-
>   friend get together in secret! Help them
>   cheat on her man, skirt him however
>   they can!
> Sometimes, a lover gets blocked and boxed
>   out. Have him try different tactics: flat-
>   tery, verbal abuse, croon a sad song to
>   the door.

Be content with those tears, and no one'll call
You a murderer. Your torch shouldn't produce
flames for a funeral pyre!"

—Haec ego; movit Amor gemmatas aureus alas,
   et mihi "propositum perfice" dixit "opus." 40

■ ■ ■

That's what I said. Love spread His wings, a halo appearing, glittering. "Fine," He allowed. "Finish the work you propose."

∎ ∎ ∎

Ad mea, decepti iuvenes, praecepta venite,
   quos suus ex omni parte fefellit amor.
Discite sanari, per quem didicistis amare;
   una manus vobis vulnus opemque feret.

Terra salutares herbas, eademque nocentes   45
   nutrit, et urticae proxima saepe rosa est.
Vulnus in Herculeo quae quondam fecerat
      hoste,
   vulneris auxilium Pelias hasta tulit.

Sed, quaecumque viris, vobis quoque dicta,
      puellae,
   credite: diversis partibus arma damus,   50
e quibus ad vestros siquid non pertinet usus,
   attamen exemplo multa docere potest.

THE POEM

Step right up, all you naïve victims! Come to my
dictums—if you're a fool for love, or been bam-
boozled, betrayed! Learn to recover now from
the teacher you learned how to love from! One
and the selfsame hand brings both the pain and
the cure:

> Earth produces herbs that are wholesome;
>   the same Earth produces toxins.
> Nettles are found often right next to a rose.
> Telephus once took a hit and got hurt by
>   the spear of Achilles; yet that very spear
>   brought him relief from the hurt.

Oh, and ladies? Please be aware that when I say
"men" here, *you're* my audience, too: I supply
arms to both sides. You may find some things
I say irrelevant; fine, but do give them thought:
you can learn much from analogy, too.[13]

Utile propositum est saevas extinguere flammas,
    nec servum vitii pectus habere sui.
Vixisset Phyllis, si me foret usa magistro,   **55**
    et per quod novies, saepius isset iter;
nec moriens Dido summa vidisset ab arce
    Dardanias vento vela dedisse rates,
nec dolor armasset contra sua viscera matrem,
    quae socii damno sanguinis ulta virum est. **60**
Arte mea Tereus, quamvis Philomela placeret,
    per facinus fieri non meruisset avis.
Da mihi Pasiphaen, iam tauri ponet amorem;
    da Phaedran, Phaedrae turpis abibit amor.

One good idea is to kill off the flames of your passion—cold turkey. Break the addiction you feel! Don't let your heart be a slave.[14]

Phyllis would have survived if she had had me for her teacher! Rather than only nine times, she'd have kept going to check.

Dido wouldn't have died when she saw, from her citadel's summit, treacherous Trojan ships missing—they'd gone with the wind.

Nor would betrayal have radicalized that mother to kill her babies (blood that they'd shared!) just so she'd have her revenge.

My methods would've stopped Tereus, though he craved Philomela, getting turned into a bird—that was the price for his rape.

Give me Pasiphae! She'll soon be getting over her bull-love.

Give me Phaedra! Her sick love will be on its way out.

Crede Parin nobis, Helenen Menelaus
        habebit,   65
    nec manibus Danais Pergama victa cadent.
Impia si nostros legisset Scylla libellos,
    haesisset capiti purpura, Nise, tuo.

Me duce damnosas, homines, compescite curas,
    rectaque cum sociis me duce navis eat.   70
Naso legendus erat tum, quom didicistis
        amare;
    idem nunc vobis Naso legendus erit.
Publicus assertor dominis suppressa levabo
    pectora: vindictae quisque favete suae.

¡Te precor incipiens, adsit tua laurea nobis,   75
    carminis et medicae, Phoebe, repertor opis!
Tu pariter vati, pariter succurre medenti:
    utraque tutelae subdita cura tuae est.

・ ・ ・

Just bring Paris to me; Menelaus will hang
on to Helen! Troy won't get conquered
and fall, razed by the hands of the
Greeks.

As for that sicko, Scylla: if she had just
read through this guidebook, Nisus's
famed purple hair would've remained
on his head.[15]

People, arrest the course of this destructive addiction! I am your leader, your guide; let's get this crew sailing straight.

Back when you were learning to love, you had to read Ovid. Now, nothing's changed; you will have to read Ovid again. I will emancipate, liberate, hearts in thrall to a lover, bring them relief. So, embrace freedom—the moment is here!

Phoebus, I pray to You as I start! May Your laurel assist me, Lord and inventor of song, founder of medical help! Equally succor Your prophet, and equally succor his healing! Both of these two roles fall under Your guardianship.

■ ■ ■

DUM LICET, et modici tangunt praecordia motus,
    si piget, in primo limine siste pedem.   80
Opprime, dum nova sunt, subiti mala semina
      morbi,
    et tuus incipiens ire resistat equus.
Nam mora dat vires; teneras mora percoquit
      uvas,
    et validas segetes quae fuit herba, facit.

Quae praebet latas arbor spatiantibus umbras, 85
    quo posita est primum tempore, virga fuit;
Tum poterat manibus summa tellure revelli;
    nunc stat in inmensum viribus aucta suis.

Quale sit id quod amas, celeri circumspice
      mente,
    et tua laesuro subtrahe colla iugo.   90
Principiis obsta: serò medicina paratur,

WHILE YOU STILL CAN, when the butterflies tickling your stomach are just so-so, if everything starts feeling wrong—just don't set foot in that door! Crush, while they're new, those evil seeds at the onset of illness. Just as it's starting to bolt, halt your horse. Have it hold back. Waiting, you see, breeds strength:

> Waiting ripens sour grapes, and matures them.
> Waiting transforms little buds into a field full of crops.

That tree over there offering plenty of shade to people out walking? When first planted, it was only a sapling, a twig. Then—back then—bare hands could've ripped it out of the topsoil. Now it's gigantic. It's grown huge and increased in its strength.

Take a hard look, for a second, at what you're actually in love with. Get out from under the yoke. Stop it from crushing your neck.

Stop the onset! Because once it's begun, it's too late to seek treatment. Problems get worse

quom mala per longas convaluere moras.
Sed propera, nec te venturas differ in horas:
   qui non est hodie, cras minus aptus erit.

Verba dat omnis amor, reperitque alimenta
     morando;   **95**
   optima vindictae proxima quaeque dies.

Flumina pauca vides de magnis fontibus orta;
   plurima collectis multiplicantur aquis.
Si citò sensisses, quantum peccare parares,
   non tegeres vultus cortice, Myrrha, tuos.   **100**

Vidi ego, quod fuerat primò sanabile, vulnus
   dilatum longae damna tulisse morae.

if you keep ignoring and putting them off. So, get moving! Don't find an excuse to procrastinate further. "He who is not ready today, shall—come tomorrow—be less."

Love is a scam—every time, every case— and it thrives on postponement. Every tomorrow that comes brings your best chance to break free.[16]

A scam? Ouch! Didn't Ovid just tell Cupid the opposite? This is our first hint that in this poem, our author will be exaggerating for effect.

Rare is the river you'll find full strength at
    its headwater sources. Most rivers, far
    and away, deepen by gathering streams.
Myrrha, if you'd been quick to realize
    what a sin you were planning, hands
    would be hiding your face—not the
    hard bark of a tree.[17]

I've seen conditions which could have been treated at first, take a turn and cause complications, because treatment kept getting put off.

Sed, quia delectat Veneris decerpere fructum,
    dicimus assidue "cras quoque fiet idem."
Interea tacitae serpunt in viscera flammae,   105
    et mala radices altius arbor agit.

Si tamen auxilii perierunt tempora primi,
    et vetus in capto pectore sedit amor,
Maius opus superest; sed non, quia serior
        aegro
    advocor, ille mihi destituendus erit.   110

Quam laesus fuerat, partem Poeantius heros
    certa debuerat praesecuisse manu;
Post tamen hic multos sanatus creditur annos
    supremam bellis imposuisse manum.

Qui modo nascentes properabam pellere
        morbos,   115
    admoveo tardam nunc tibi lentus opem.
Aut nova, si possis, sedare incendia temptes,
    aut ubi per vires procubuere suas.
Dum furor in cursu est, currenti cede furori;
    difficiles aditus impetus omnis habet.   120

"Gathering Venus's fruits"—having sex—is fun. That's the problem. We're always telling ourselves, "I'll just continue like this."[18] Flames, meanwhile, are snaking unnoticed all through our bodies. Roots of the evil tree work themselves deeper within.

Suppose that initial window for treatment has closed, and you missed it: love's become chronic, persists, lingering long in your breast. More work, then, is involved. Still, though it's late to be calling on me, I'll never say no, never give up on your case.

For Philoctetes—Poeas's heroic son— amputation would've been best: just lop off all that gangrenous flesh. Nevertheless, it all healed (so we're told), even if many years later. Then, his surefire hand ended the long Trojan War.[19]

I—who was just in a rush to stave off your disease at its onset—now, I'll take my time. Here comes my slow-release cure.

You should extinguish a fire the moment it breaks out, or, if you can't, then wait until it burns itself out. When a mania is raging, step back and allow it to rage. Every erratic impulse

Stultus, ab obliquo qui quom descendere possit,
    pugnat in adversas ire natator aquas.
Impatiens animus nec adhuc tractabilis artem
    respuit, atque odio verba monentis habet.

Adgrediar melius tum, quom sua
      vulnera tangi   125
    iam sinet, et veris vocibus aptus erit.
¿Quis matrem, nisi mentis inops, in funere nati
    flere vetet? Non hoc illa monenda loco est.
Quom dederit lacrimas animumque impleverit
      aegrum,
    ille dolor verbis emoderandus erit.   130
Temporis ars medicina fere est:
      data tempore prosunt,
    et data non apto tempore vina nocent.
Quin etiam accendas vitia irritesque vetando,
    temporibus si non adgrediare suis.

Ergo, ubi visus eris nostra medicabilis arte,   135
    fac monitis fugias otia prima meis.

frustrates an easy approach. Likewise, the swimmer's a fool who could "ferry" across at a slant but fights the current instead, struggling to make it upstream. Just so, a heart that can't take it and isn't yet ready for treatment scorns therapeutic advice, irked at his counselor's words.

I'll do better to make my approach only after he'll let his wounds be touched, when he's more open to hearing the truth. Who but a fool would stop a mother from grieving at her son's funeral? That's not the time, that's not the place for advice. After she has shed all her tears, and hence salved and started to mend her broken heart, that's when words put an end to the pain.

Medicine's really the art of timing. Wine, for example, dosed at the right time does good, while at the wrong time, does harm. Worse, you can actually aggravate illness by trying to repress it. Some inflammations increase if you attack them too soon.

Ergo, once you decide for yourself that my system can help you, follow my orders. Rule one:

Never have "nothing to do."

Haec, ut ames, faciunt; haec, ut fecere, tuentur;
    haec sunt iucundi causa cibusque mali.
Otia si tollas, periere Cupidinis arcus,
    contemptaeque iacent et sine luce faces.   **140**
Quam platanus vino gaudet, quam pōpulus
        unda,
    et quam limosa canna palustris humo,
Tam Venus otia amat; qui finem quaeris amoris,

    cedit amor rebus: res age, tutus eris.
Languor, et inmodici sub nullo
        vindice somni,   **145**
    aleaque, et multo tempora quassa mero
eripiunt omnes animo sine vulnere nervos;
    affluit incautis insidiosus Amor.
Desidiam puer ille sequi solet, odit agentes:
    da vacuae menti, quo teneatur, opus.   **150**

Sunt fora, sunt leges, sunt quos tuearis amici:

"Nothing to do" makes you fall in love, and then keeps you a captive. Downtime stimulates and makes the infection feel good. Take away downtime, and voilà—right there, Cupid's arrows are pointless. So is His torch. It'll go out and just lie there, ignored. Just as the plane tree thrills to wine,[20] as the poplar loves water, and as the marshy reed thrives in the muck and the mud, that's how much Venus loves "nothing to do." If you want to end love, then, love—recall—takes a backseat to things.

Do something, and you'll be safe. Lying around, unlimited sleep where there's nothing to wake you, bingeing on gambling and games, booze which is addling your brain. . . . All of this saps the strength of your mind (without leaving a wound, though). It's how insidious Love seeps imperceptibly in. Sitting around attracts that boy; He's repelled by the active.

So, when you're bored, give your mind interesting work to do. Law courts exist; there are laws, there are friends, whose fate you can plead for.

vade per urbanae splendida castra togae.

Vel tu sanguinei iuvenalia munera Martis
   suscipe: deliciae iam tibi terga dabunt.

Ecce, fugax Parthus, magni nova causa
     triumphi,   **155**
   iam videt in campis Caesaris arma suis.
Vince Cupidineas pariter Parthasque sagittas,
   et refer ad patrios bina tropaea deos.

Ut semel Aetola Venus est a cuspide laesa,
   mandat amatori bella gerenda suo.   **160**
¿Quaeritur, Aegisthus quare sit factus
     adulter?
   In promptu causa est: desidiosus erat.
Pugnabant alii tardis apud Ilion armis;
   transtulerat vires Graecia tota suas.

Go out and fight on campaign—
wearing a toga, downtown.

Or, as a young man should,

heed the call of duty.

In combat—blood everywhere—fun and games
soon beat a hasty retreat.
   (Speaking of which, the flight-prone Parthians—they'll be our latest triumph—already
see Caesar's great troops on their plains.[21] You
can blunt Parthian arrows as well as the arrows
of Cupid, both simultaneously, bringing *two*
trophies back home.)

One little scratch Diomedes gave Her sent
   Venus packing—made Her give up and
   go home, leaving the fighting to Mars.
Want to know why Aegisthus became
   a home-wrecker? Simple: that draft
   dodger was bored, idle and sitting around.
   Everyone else was bogged down fighting the long war off in Troy, where all

Sive operam bellis vellet dare, nulla gerebat,   **165**
    sive foro, vacuum litibus Argos erat.
Quod potuit, ne nil illic ageretur, amavit.
    Sic venit ille puer, sic puer ille manet.

Rura quoque oblectant animos studiumque
    colendi;
    quaelibet huic curae cedere cura potest.   **170**

Colla iube domitos oneri supponere tauros,
    sauciet ut duram vomer aduncus humum;
Obrue versata Cerealia semina terra,
    quae tibi cum multo faenore reddat ager.
Aspice curvatos pomorum pondere ramos,   **175**

of Greece had shipped off its mobilized
men. What could he do? Go enlist in
a war? No, Argos didn't have one. Go
be a lawyer downtown? No, all the
dockets were clear. So, to have something to do, he did what he could: he
(*winking*)—got busy.[22] That's how the
little guy comes, that's how the little guy
stays.

Many find life on the land, and farming, another great option.

Farm life can easily fix any
fixation you have.

Cow bulls into submission! Bully them to load
up their necks and gash the hard ground till it
splits, hooked on the blade of a plow. Turn up
the earth! Then, bury your cereal seeds—and
then stomp 'em. They're an investment: the land
yields an amazing return.

Now picture branches bending under the
weight of their apples. See how they strain not

ut sua, quod peperit, vix ferat arbor onus;
Aspice labentes iucundo murmure rivos;
   aspice tondentes fertile gramen oves.

Ecce, petunt rupes praeruptaque saxa capellae:
   iam referent haedis ubera plena suis.   180
Pastor inaequali modulatur harundine carmen,
   nec desunt comites, sedula turba, canes.
Parte sonant alia silvae mugitibus altae,
   et queritur vitulum mater abesse suum.
¿Quid, quom compositos fugiunt examina
      fumos,   185
   ut relevent dempti vimina curva favi?

Poma dat autumnus: formosa est messibus
      aestas;
   ver praebet flores: igne levatur hiems.
Temporibus certis maturam rusticus uvam
   deligit, et nudo sub pede musta fluunt;   190
Temporibus certis desectas alligat herbas,
   et tonsam raro pectine verrit humum.

to drop babies that they themselves bore. Now picture babbling brooks. Aren't they nice? The sound is so pleasant. . . . Now picture sheep in lush fields, grazing and clipping the grass.

On that note, goats are now headed to find jagged crags, and soon they'll be bringing their kids udders distended with milk. Now a shepherd's playing a melody on his reed pipe, while dogs—man's best friend—sit around spellbound and watch. Elsewhere, a woodland forest is echoing mooing, because a mama cow can't find her calf, wailing it's time to come home. Then there are bees; they'll scatter at fumigant, swarming, so you can loot their wicker skep domes, keeping the honey and combs.

Autumn brings apples, summertime's gorgeous with wheat fields, and springtime offers you flowers in bloom; winter is tempered with fire. Seasonally, when it's time, your man of the country will gather ripened grapes in, and the juice oozes between his bare toes. Seasonally, when it's time, he'll harvest the wheat and he'll bind it. Then, he'll go harrow the ground, using a rake with wide teeth.

Ipse potes riguis plantam deponere in hortis,
　　ipse potes rivos ducere lenis aquae.
Venerit insitio; fac ramum ramus adoptet,　　**195**
　　stetque peregrinis arbor operta comis.
Quom semel haec animum coepit mulcere
　　　voluptas,
　　debilibus pinnis irritus exit Amor.

Vel tu venandi studium cole: saepe recessit
　　turpiter a Phoebi victa sorore Venus.　　**200**

Nunc leporem pronum catulo sectare sagaci,
　　nunc tua frondosis retia tende iugis,
aut pavidos terre varia formidine cervos,
　　aut cadat adversa cuspide fossus aper.
Nocte fatigatum somnus, non cura puellae,　　**205**
　　excipit, et pingui membra quiete levat.

Lenius est studium, studium tamen, alite capta
　　aut lino aut calamis praemia parva sequi,

You yourself get to plant what you like in well-watered gardens. You yourself get to choose channels, and where they should go. Grafting time? Make a branch take in and foster another. Have a tree preen in a wig, clad in expatriate leaves.

Once these pleasures begin to relax your heart and your heartache, Love's a goner. He goes fluttering off and away.

Otherwise, hunting's a hobby to cultivate.

Venus has often turned tail and shamefully fled after Diana prevails![23]

Day number one? Have your bloodhound chase a scampering rabbit. Day number two? Set up traps out among trees in the hills. Go out and terrorize jumpy deer with a predator decoy, or stop a boar dead in its tracks, felled by a thrust of your spear. That way, exhausted at night, it's sleep—and not thoughts of your girlfriend— that'll embrace you. You'll find deep and re-storative . . . sleep.

Easier options—not as tough, but they're options—include trapping birds, and hunting

vel, quae piscis edax avido male devoret ore,
    abdere sub parvis aera recurva cibis.   **210**
Aut his aut aliis, donec dediscis amare,
    ipse tibi furtim decipiendus eris.

Tu tantùm, quamvis firmis retinebere vinclis,
    i procul, et longas carpere perge vias.

Flebis, et occurret desertae nomen amicae,   **215**
    stabit et in media pes tibi saepe via.
Sed quanto minus ire voles, magis ire memento;
    perfer, et invitos currere coge pedes.
Nec pluvias opta, nec te peregrina morentur
    sabbata, nec damnis Allia nota suis;   **220**
Nec quot transieris, sed quot tibi, quaere,
      supersint
    milia; nec, maneas ut prope, finge moras.
Tempora nec numera, nec crebrò respice
      Romam,

a littler prize using nets or a long, sticky pole, or you can slip metal hooks under bait for fish to come gulp down eagerly in their mouths. (Greed's a disastrous choice.) Do one of these, or do something else, until you unlearn love. You have to trick yourself—*trick* yourself tricking yourself.

So, no matter how strong the chains that're holding you back, just:

> *Get out and go far away.*
> *Take a long trip out of town.*

Yes, you'll cry, and the name of the girl you abandoned will haunt you. Often, you'll stop and think twice, think about turning around. No. When you really don't feel like going, that's when to double down. Hang on! Power through, make your feet pick up the pace. Don't wish for rain, and don't let the sabbath (a day off) delay you. Allia's not an excuse, tragic a day though it is.[24] Don't ask how many miles you've gone, but how many more there are. Don't fake an excuse, either, for sticking around. Don't check the calendar. Don't keep looking over

35

sed fuge: tutus adhuc Parthus ab hoste
    fuga est.

Dura aliquis praecepta vocet mea;
    dura fatemur   225
  esse; sed ut valeas, multa dolenda feres.
Saepe bibi sucos, quamvis invitus, amaros
  aeger, et oranti mensa negata mihi.
Ut corpus redimas, ferrum patieris et ignes,
  arida nec sitiens ora levabis aqua: 230
¿Ut valeas animo, quicquam tolerare negabis?
  At pretium pars haec corpore maius habet.

Sed tamen est artis tristissima ianua nostrae,
  et labor est unus tempora prima pati.
¿Aspicis ut prensos urant iuga prima
    iuvencos,   235
  et nova velocem cingula laedat equum?
Forsitan a laribus patriis exire pigebit;
  sed tamen exibis; deinde redire voles.

your shoulder back at Rome. No, flee! Make like our Parthian foe.

Some might say my prescriptions are hard. They are. I admit it. There's no gain without pain. Want to get better? Get tough!

Many times, I've choked syrupy medicines down—they're disgusting—when I was sick; I've withheld food from myself. It was rough.

Think: to rehab your body, you'll put up with cutting and burning—even refusing to drink water when dying of thirst. Hence, for emotional health, what treatment could you say no to? Mental well-being is more useful than physical health.

Nevertheless, it's the door that's the hardest part of my program. Mainly, your job is to get through day number one, and day two. Don't you see how, at first, a yoke chafes bulls' necks when they're starting out? How a saddle that's new blisters and rubs your horse raw?

Probably you'll have a tough time getting going ("it's the place I grew up in!"). Still, though, you'll make it—you will!

Nec te Lar patrius, sed amor revocabit amicae,
    praetendens culpae splendida verba tuae. **240**

Quom semel exieris, centum solacia curae
    et rus et comites et via longa dabit.
Nec satis esse putes discedere; lentus abesto,
    dum perdat vires sitque sine igne cinis.
Quod nisi firmata properâris mente reverti, **245**
    inferet arma tibi saeva rebellis Amor,
Quidquid et afueris, avidus sitiensque redibis,
    et spatium damno cesserit omne tuo.

Viderit, Haemoniae siquis mala pabula terrae
    et magicas artes posse iuvare putat. **250**
Ista veneficii vetus est via; noster Apollo
    innocuam sacro carmine monstrat opem.
Me duce, non tumulo prodire iubebitur umbra,
    non anus infami carmine rumpet humum,

Next, you'll want to go back. Thoughts of the place you grew up in won't haunt you, though; thoughts of your girlfriend will. You'll rationalize quitting, and lie to yourself.

Once you finally get moving, you'll find a hundred distractions: countryside landscapes . . . friends . . . even the road trip itself.

Don't go thinking just leaving's enough, though. Stay gone a while, till the smoldering dies down and the embers go out. That's because if you go back too quick and you haven't recovered, Love will flare up and resume doggedly gunning for you. Despite all your being away, therefore, the cravings will hit you when you get back—so the trip totally wasted your time.

Best to think twice if you're counting on help from the sorcerous herbals Thessaly offers, or if you think witchcraft will cure you somehow.[25] Magic—because that's what it is—is obsolete. The mystical guide of *my* song, Apollo, is teaching us *harmless* relief. On my watch, no ghosts will get summoned up from their graves, and hags will not open up hell, splitting the

non seges ex aliis alios transibit in agros,   255
   nec subito Phoebi pallidus orbis erit.
Ut solet, aequoreas ibit Tiberinus in undas;
   ut solet, in niveis Luna vehetur equis.
Nulla recantatas deponent pectora curas,
   nec fugiet vivo sulphure victus Amor.   260

¿Quid te Phasiacae iuverunt gramina terrae,
   quom cuperes patria, Colchi, manere domo?
¿Quid tibi profuerunt, Circe, Perseides herbae,
   quom sua Neritias abstulit aura rates?
Omnia fecisti, ne callidus hospes abiret: 265
   ille dedit certae lintea plena fugae.
Omnia fecisti, ne te ferus ureret ignis:
   longus et invito pectore sedit Amor.
Vertere tu poteras homines in mille figuras;
   non poteras animi vertere iura tui.   270

earth with a spell. Crops won't go crossing over into neighboring fields, and sunlight won't blanch and grow dim, sallow and pale, on a whim. Just like always, the Tiber will flow out into the sea, and just like always, the moon won't disappear in eclipse. No hexes or spells will make any hearts renounce their fixations, nor will a whiff of brimstone chase Love away in defeat.

Please. What good did your Georgian botanicals do you, Medea, when you were hoping to stay home in your father's abode? Circe, what help, per se, were your birthright wortplant concoctions, if just a nice little breeze whisked your Ulysses away?[26] Try as you might, you couldn't dissuade your "houseguest" from leaving. Hell-bent on fleeing, he snuck out and away—with full sail. Try as you might, you couldn't help getting engulfed in the blazing fire; no, Love set in, living rent-free in your head. No, you could change human beings into thousands of shapes, but you couldn't change or transform laws holding sway in the heart. Worse (so we're told), Ithaca's hero was

Diceris his etiam, quom iam discedere vellet,
    Dulichium verbis detinuisse ducem:

"Non ego, quod primò, memini, sperare
      solebam,
    iam precor, ut coniunx tu meus esse velis;
et tamen, ut coniunx essem tua,
      digna videbar,   275
    quod dea, quod magni filia Solis eram.
Ne properes, oro; spatium pro munere posco;
    ¿quid minus optari per mea vota potest?
Et freta mota vides, et debes illa timere:
    utilior velis postmodo ventus erit.   280
¿Quae tibi causa fugae? Non hīc nova Troia
      resurgit,
    non aliquis socios rursus ad arma vocat.
Hīc amor et pax est, in qua male vulneror una,
    tutaque sub regno terra futura tuo est."

Illa loquebatur, navem solvebat Ulixes;   285
    irrita cum velis verba tulere Noti.

anxious to *just get going already!*—but you begged him to stay, saying this:

> "Please! I'm not asking—I know, I did hope it at first, I remember—now I'm not asking you to want to get married to me. (True, I did really think I'd have made you a suitable wife, since I am a goddess myself, child of the almighty Sun.) Please don't go so soon. I beg you for time, as a present. Is there anything less? What smaller thing could I ask?
>
> Also, you see how the sea is choppy and rough; you should fear it. Later, the wind will become better for filling your sails. Why are you running away? There's no new Troy in the offing here, no call to start up mobilization again. Here, there's love and there's peace, and there's only one casualty here: me. All this land will enjoy safety. You'll rule it as king. . . ."

While she was speaking, Ulysses was freeing his ship from its moorings. Gales, it seems, drowned out her pleas, blowing 'em off—just like him.

Ardet et assuetas Circe decurrit ad artes,
　　nec tamen est illis attenuatus amor.
Ergo, quisquis opem nostra tibi poscis
　　　　ab arte,
　　　　deme veneficiis carminibusque fidem.　　　**290**

Si te causa potens domina retinebit in Urbe,
　　accipe, consilium quod sit in Urbe meum.
Optimus ille sui vindex, laedentia pectus
　　vincula qui rupit, dedoluitque semel.
Sed cui tantum animi est, illum mirabor
　　　　et ipse,　　　　　　　　　　　　　　**295**
　　　　et dicam "monitis non eget iste meis."
Tu mihi, qui, quod amas, aegre dediscis
　　　　amare,
　　　　nec potes, et velles posse, docendus eris.
Saepe refer tecum sceleratae facta puellae,
　　et pone ante oculos omnia damna tuos:　　**300**

All hot and bothered, Circe fell back on her typical arts, but those tricks couldn't dispel Love, couldn't rid her of Him. Ergo—whoever you are—if you're looking to my arts for help, then:

> *Place not your faith in spells,*
> *abracadabras, and charms.*

If some powerful cause keeps you bound to our mistress, the City, well—here you go; this is my City-specific advice. Your best chance to get free is to break the destructive addiction chaining your heart and endure all the withdrawal pains at once. (Even I'll be amazed at the man who can actually do that, though, and I'll say that *that* man needs no ideas from me.) You, who have trouble unlearning to love your current obsession—want to, but can't—well, you're going to have to be taught. Ruminate, often, on all the bad things that minx put you through, and

> *fixate on all that you lost, fixate*
> *on all that she cost.*

"Illud et illud habet, nec ea contenta rapina est:
    sub titulum nostros misit avara lares.
¡Sic mihi iuravit, sic me iurata fefellit,
    ante suas quotiens passa iacere fores!
Diligit ipsa alios, a me fastidit amari;   305

Now, fixating on anything sounds like a bad idea, but there's a logic to it. Ovid just advised us to go cold turkey; now he'll tell us exactly how *we'll power through withdrawal symptoms—namely, by brooding on the financial costs of our failed relationship. Those thoughts will in turn bring to mind all the times we were or felt emotionally cheated or betrayed. To illustrate the thought process, Ovid channels the mindset of a man who's been badly damaged in a breakup. He's angrily recalling all the material possessions his ex wound up with.*

Think:

She got that . . . she got *that* . . . and she's not just happy with stealing *that*; that gold-digger's forced me to sell my whole *house*! *That's* when she swore we'd meet up; *that's* when she went back on her promise . . . leading me on all those times . . . freezing me out at the door. *Other* men? They're just *great*, but she's "too good"

¡institor, heu, noctes, quas mihi non dat,
    habet!"
Haec tibi per totos inacescant omnia sensus:
    haec refer, hinc odii semina quaere tui.
Atque utinam possis etiam facundus in illis
    esse; dole tantùm, sponte disertus eris.   310

for my loving. Hell, the delivery man gets
all the nights that I don't!

Let all these thoughts embitter your mind and
sour your feelings. Brood on them. In them,
you'll find seeds you can grow into hate. In
them, I also hope you'll become a fiery speaker.
Just feel aggrieved, and you'll find eloquence all
on your own.

Philosophers in every age pride them-
selves on "seeing things as they really
are" and "calling things by their true
names"—no hypocrisy for them! Such un-
varnished truth may make for great phi-
losophy, but it's comically disastrous in
relationships. A couple of generations be-
fore Ovid, the enigmatic poet Lucretius
had taken these ideas to their logical ex-
treme in his philosophical poem On the
Nature of Things. *In a notorious passage*
at the end of book 4, Lucretius had rec-
ommended in earnest the very woman-
demonizing strategies that Ovid is about

Haeserat in quadam nuper mea cura puella:
    conveniens animo non erat illa meo.
Curabar propriis aeger Podalirius herbis,
    (et, fateor, medicus turpiter aeger eram):
Profuit assidue vitiis insistere amicae,   315
    idque mihi factum saepe salubre fuit.
"¡Quàm mala" dicebam "nostrae sunt crura
      puellae!"
    (Nec tamen, ut vere confiteamur, erant.)
"¡Bracchia quàm non sunt nostrae formosa
      puellae!"
    (Et tamen, ut vere confiteamur, erant.)   320
"¡Quàm brevis est!" (Nec erat), "¡Quàm
      multum poscit amantem!"
    Haec odio venit maxima causa meo.

Et mala sunt vicina bonis; errore sub illo
    pro vitio virtus crimina saepe tulit.
Qua potes, in peius dotes deflecte puellae,   325

*to recommend here. Is Ovid in earnest,
too? Or is it all parody?*

Not long ago, I developed a crush on this girl
that I knew, who, personality-wise, wasn't the
best match for me. I—Podalirius!—self-
medicated with my own cures, though. (Yes, it's
ironic, I know: sadly, your doctor was sick).[27]
One thing that helped was constantly harping
on all of my ex's flaws, because that, once I did,
often would bring me relief. Here's what I'd say:
"Whoa . . . look at my girlfriend's terrible an-
kles." (That wasn't actually true, since they were
perfectly fine.) "Look at my girlfriend's arms,
and how they're *so* unattractive." (That wasn't
actually true, since they were perfectly fine.)
"Look at how short she is." (Though she
wasn't.) "Look at how needy." (That one—her
constant demands—actually did make me hate.)
   Another is that "bad" is so close to "good."
Often, we'll see a virtue get criticized, since
people mistake it for vice. So where you can,

minimize and belittle your ex's best features.

iudiciumque brevi limite falle tuum.
"Turgida," si plena est, si fusca est, "nigra"
    vocetur;
    in gracili, "macies" crimen habere potest.
Et poterit dici "petulans," quae rustica non
    est;
    et poterit dici "rustica," siqua proba est.   330
Quin etiam, quacumque caret tua femina dote,
    hanc moveat, blandis usque precare sonis.
Exige uti cantet, siqua est sine voce puella:
    fac saltet, nescit siqua movere manum.
¿Barbara sermone est? Fac tecum multa
    loquatur.   335
    ¿Non didicit chordas tangere? Posce
    lyram.
¿Durius incedit? Fac inambulet. ¿Omne
    papillae
    pectus habent? Vitium fascia nulla tegat.
Si male dentata est, narra, quod rideat, illi;
    ¿mollibus est oculis? Quod fleat illa,
    refer.   340
Proderit et subito, quom se non finxerit ulli,

Blur and exploit the fine line, telling yourself
that it's true. If she's curvaceous, then call her
"enlarged." Say she's "dark" if she's tawny.
"Starving" can be an insult when a girl's slender
and fit. "Brash" is the thing to call a girl who
isn't just mousy. "Mousy" is the thing to call
one who is actually sweet.

Go even further. Whatever talent your ex is
lacking, nag her to show it off (always with flat-
tering words). Urge her to sing if the woman
that you're with has a voice that's no good, or
get her to dance if she is clueless about how to
move her arms. Can't speak Latin correctly?
Engage her in long conversations. Doesn't
know how to play chords? Have someone bring
her a lyre. Walks all weird? Then go for a walk.
Her breasts are all over, filling her chest? It's a
flaw; ask her to not wear a bra. Teeth in bad
shape? Then tell her a story or joke. Get her
laughing. Overemotional, cries? Share some sad
news. Make her sob.

Something else that'll work is surprise. Before she's put her face on,

ad dominam celeres mane tulisse gradus.

Auferimur cultu; gemmis auroque teguntur
    omnia; pars minima est ipsa puella sui.
Saepe ubi sit quod ames, inter tam multa
        requiras;   345
    decipit hac oculos aegide dives Amor.
Improvisus ades; deprendes tutus inermem:
    infelix vitiis excidet illa suis.
Non tamen huic nimium praecepto credere
        tutum est:
    fallit enim multos forma sine arte decens. 350

Tum quoque, compositis quom collinet ora
        venenis,
    ad dominae vultus (nec pudor obstet) eas:
Pyxidas invenies et rerum mille colores,
    et fluere in tepidos oesypa lapsa sinus.
Illa tuas redolent, Phineu, medicamina
        mensas: 355
    non semel hinc stomacho nausea facta
        meo est.

*go in the morning and drop in on her,
all unannounced.*

Hair and makeup seduce and mislead us, and
jewelry disguises all: of a girl, the least part is the
actual girl. Often, you'd wonder, with all that
stuff, where the thing that you love is; glittering camouflage dazzles our eyes—when she's
rich. Come to her place without warning; you'll
catch her unarmed and defenseless. You'll be
fine, but the girl's doomed by her blemishes.
Sad.

(Still, it's unwise to put too much stock in this
recommendation. Natural beauty, you see, stuns
many men—makeup-free.)

Also, sometime when she's smearing her face
with her poisonous products, go get a look at
your belle. Don't be embarrassed. Go in. There
you'll find jars, and things, and zillions of col-
ors, and . . . oozing sheep-grease—warmed by
her skin—trickling into her chest.

Phineus, those concealers remind me of *your*
dinner table! More than just once, I've felt sick
to my stomach from them.[28]

Nunc tibi, quae medio Veneris praestemus in
    usu,
  eloquar: ex omni est parte fugandus Amor.
Multa quidem ex illis pudor est mihi dicere;
    sed tu
  ingenio verbis concipe plura meis. . . .   **360**

ERGO, UBI CONCUBITUS et opus iuvenale petetur,
  et prope promissae tempora noctis erunt, **400**
gaudia ne dominae, pleno si corpore sumes,
  te capiant, ineas quamlibet ante velim;

Now, since love must be totally banished and out of the picture, let's talk sex. I'll explain what you should do in the act. Many ideas I'm embarrassed to say explicitly, so . . . use your brain and infer more than I'm saying in words. . . .

Before saying it in words, Ovid inserts a page-long rebuttal to claims that his poetry is obscene. Since the digression is technical and distracting, I have moved it to an appendix. When the poem resumes, a significant darkening of tone and tactics is evident. Ovid will now begin recommending strategies equivalent to chopping hands off thieves: effective, perhaps, but deliberately offensive and evil. Does he really mean any of this?

. . . SO THEN, WHEN SEX (because that's what young people do) is requested, once it's starting to get close to the time for your date, so that enjoying your lady won't hook and entrap you, because your body feels ready to burst,

go hump a random girl first.

quamlibet invenias, in qua tua prima voluptas
    desinat: a prima proxima segnis erit.   **404**

Et pudet, et dicam: Venerem quoque iunge
    figura   **407**
    qua minime iungi quamque decere putas.

Nec labor efficere est: rarae sibi vera fatentur,
    et nihil est, quod se dedecuisse putent.   **410**
Tunc etiam iubeo totas aperire fenestras,
    turpiaque admisso membra notare die.
At simul ad metas venit finita voluptas,
    lassaque cum tota corpora mente iacent,
Dum piget, et malles nullam tetigisse
    puellam,   **415**
    tacturusque tibi non videare diu,
tunc animo signa, quaecumque in corpore
    menda est,
    luminaque in vitiis illius usque tene.

That's my advice; find a random girl and use her
to expend your first round of pleasure. After
that, round number two will be tough.

Here's an embarrassing one, but I'll say it:

*Adopt an outrageous sex position — an
abnormal, unflattering one.*

(That isn't hard, by the way, because pretty
much every girl out there flatters herself that
nothing looks bad on her; it's rare for them to
admit the truth.)

That's not all; I advise you to also open the
curtains. Once the light's flooding in, notice
how unsightly she looks.

Lastly, as soon as your pleasure's expended
and come to its finish, and you're lying there
drained — physically, mentally shot —, while
you're disgusted and wishing you'd never
touched a girl, and you're thinking you probably won't touch a girl anytime soon, that's
when to note any imperfections you see on her
body. Rivet your gaze on her flaws. Make
mental notes of each one.

Forsitan haec aliquis (nam sunt quoque) parva
     vocabit,
     sed, quae non prosunt singula,
          multa iuvant.   420
Parva necat morsu spatiosum vipera taurum;
     a cane non magno saepe tenetur aper.
Tu tantùm numero pugna, praeceptaque in
     unum
     contrahe: de multis grandis acervus erit.
Sed quoniam totidem mores totidemque
     figurae,   425
     non sunt iudiciis omnia danda meis.
Quo tua non possunt offendi pectora facto,
     forsitan hoc alio iudice crimen erit.
Ille quod obscenas in aperto corpore partes
     viderat, in cursu qui fuit, haesit amor;   430
Ille quod a Veneris rebus surgente puella
     vidit in inmundo signa pudenda toro.

Someone might say that that's silly ("they're small!")—which is, in fact, true—but things that are useless themselves, little by little add up. Vipers are small, but a bite from one will kill an enormous bull, while often a huge boar's held in check by a dog.[29] So, just be sure to seek safety in numbers. Compile all my rules, and integrate them: out of steps, far-reaching systems emerge.

Still, because preferences come in as many styles as our bodies, not every preference will track *my* tastes 100 percent. Something can happen which, to your mind, just isn't offensive; somebody else may well find that it crosses the line:

One man glimpsed a girl's private parts
    when she opened her legs, and love—
    which was well on course—balked, and
    he couldn't perform.
One man glimpsed, when his girl got up
    from the bed after they'd had sex, an
    embarrassing wet spot that was staining
    the sheets.

Luditis, o siquos potuerunt ista movere:
    afflarant tepidae pectora vestra faces.
Attrahat ille puer contentos fortius arcus;   **435**
    saucia maiorem turba petetis opem.
¿Quid, qui clam latuit reddente obscena
        puella,
    et vidit, quae mos ipse videre vetat?
¡Di melius, quam nos moneamus talia
        quemquam!
    Ut prosint, non sunt expedienda tamen.   **440**

Hortor et ut pariter binas habeatis amicas
    (fortior est, plures siquis habere potest):

secta bipertitò quom mens discurrit utròque,
    alterius vires subtrahit alter amor.
Grandia per multos tenuantur flumina rivos, **445**
    saevaque [*Merkel:* †haesaque† *Kenney*]
    diducto stipite flamma perit.

You're all just poseurs—not really in love—if *that* could upset you. Torches without any warmth caused all the heat you might feel. Sounds like our little boy ought to rearm, pull hard on his bow, and *fire!* for real. You'll soon look for relief for your wound.

What of the man who hid when his girlfriend was voiding her privates, secretly watching a scene normal behavior precludes? Gods! Far be it from me to suggest an idea along those lines. Sure, it may actually work; still, it's just better suppressed.

Here's another suggestion:

*Juggle a couple of partners.**

See, when the mind is torn between two desires, and it's scrambling—longing—for both, the one cancels the other one out: As they split off into many a stream, mighty rivers lose muscle. Spread out the logs, and the fierce flames of a

---

* True heroes could, of course, manage to keep even more.

Non satis una tenet ceratas ancora puppes,
    nec satis est liquidis unicus hamus aquis.

Qui sibi iam pridem solacia bina paravit,
    iam pridem summa victor in arce fuit.   450
At tibi, qui fueris dominae male creditus uni,
    nunc saltem novus est inveniendus amor:

Pasiphaes Minos in Procride perdidit ignes;
    cessit ab Idaea coniuge victa prior.
Amphilochi frater ne Phegida semper
      amaret,   455
    Calliroe fecit parte recepta tori.
Et Parin Oenone summos tenuisset ad annos,
    si non Oebalia paelice laesa foret.
Coniugis Odrysio placuisset forma tyranno,
    sed melior clausae forma sororis erat.   460

fire go out. One single anchor will not secure a slippery cruiser. One hook won't, by itself, work in a fast-moving stream.

Once a man's already set himself up with double the comfort, *that* is the peak of success: victory, triumph, the win.

You, though, who stupidly find yourself monogamous, need to—now at least, having no choice—go find a new girl to love:

Minos's passionate love for Pasiphae died
    out with Procris.[30]
Likewise, Idaea—wife 2—ousted, for
    Phineus, wife 1.
Taking Callirhoe into his bed explains why
    Alcmaeon didn't keep loving his wife,
    Phegeus's daughter, for good.
Paris himself would've stayed with Oe-
    none "till death did them part" if Helen,
    his concubine wife, hadn't messed every-
    thing up.
Tereus would've been perfectly fine with
    his beautiful wife. Her sister, however,
    enslaved, proved a more beautiful girl.

¿Quid moror exemplis, quorum me turba
    fatigat?
  Successore novo vincitur omnis amor.
Fortius e multis mater desiderat unum,
    quam quem flens clamat "tu mihi solus
    eras."
Et, ne forte putes nova me tibi condere iura **465**
  (¡atque utinam inventi gloria nostra foret!),
Vidit ut Atrides: ¿quid enim non ille videret,
  cuius in arbitrio Graecia tota fuit?
Marte suo captam Chryseida, victor amabat;
  at senior stulte flebat ubique pater.   **470**

¿Quid lacrimas, odiose senex? Bene convenit
    illis;
  officio natam laedis, inepte, tuo.
Quam postquam reddi Calchas, ope tutus
    Achillis,
  iusserat, et patria est illa recepta domo,
"Est" ait Atrides "illius proxima forma,   **475**
  et, si prima sinat syllaba, nomen idem.

Why am I wasting my time on examples? They're all getting boring. *Every* love is displaced once a successor appears!

Mothers more bravely endure the death of one out of many children than when they mourn one, weeping, "you're all that I had."

By the way, perish the thought—if you have it—that I'm coming up with new laws for you (though I'd love taking the credit for that!). Once Agamemnon saw (because really, what did he not see? He was commander-in-chief over all Greece in the war!) Chryseis, seized in a battle he'd won, he was smitten. Still, her old dad couldn't stop weeping and carrying on . . .

(*Why are you crying, you stick-in-the-mud? They're happy together. Idiot! Getting involved is messing up your daughter's life.*[31])

. . . nevertheless, after Calchas (Achilles protected him) said she had to go back, and she'd been brought to her father's abode, then Agamemnon remarked,

There's an almost identical beauty, who—
if it weren't for the first syllable—has the

Hanc mihi, si sapiat, per se concedat Achilles;
    si minus, imperium sentiat ille meum.
Quod siquis vestrûm factum hoc accusat,
        Achivi,
    est aliquid valida sceptra tenere manu.   **480**
Nam si rex ego sum, nec mecum dormiat ulla,
    in mea Thersites regna licebit eat."

Dixit, et hanc habuit solacia magna prioris,
    et posita est curā cura repulsa novā.
Ergo, assume novas auctore Agamemnone
        flammas,   **485**
    ut tuus in bivio distineatur amor.
¿Quaeris, ubi invenias? Artes tu perlege nostras:
    plena puellarum iam tibi navis erit.
Quod siquid praecepta valent mea, siquid
        Apollo
    utile mortales perdocet ore meo,   **490**

same name.[32] So, if he's wise, let Achilles decide he should hand the girl over, making her mine. If he's not, he'll get a taste of my power.

And, if any of you disapprove of this measure, Achaeans: holding a scepter in hand means a great deal—when you're strong. I am the king, understand; and unless a girl's sleeping beside me, well, Thersites can take over my sovereign rule!

Basta! He took her—a great consolation prize for his former comfort, and new love replaced love(sickness); thus it was cured.[33]

Heed Agamemnon's model, therefore, and go get a new flame. That way your love will thin out, pulling in two ways at once.*[34]

If my ideas are effective at all, though, and if Apollo's made me His mouthpiece to share useful advice here on Earth, then, although you're

---

* Curious where you can find a new flame? Well, study my how-tos! Soon, you'll find that a whole bevy of women is yours!

quamvis infelix media torreberis Aetna,
   ¡frigidior glacie fac videare tuae!

Et sanum simula, nec, siquid forte dolebis,
   sentiat, et ride, quom tibi flendus eris.
Non ego te iubeo medias abrumpere curas: **495**
   non sunt imperii tam fera iussa mei.
Quod non es, simula, positosque imitare furores:
   sic facies vere, quod meditatus eris.
Saepe ego, ne biberem, volui dormire videri:
   dum videor, somno lumina victa dedi.   **500**
Deceptum risi, qui se simulârat amare,
   in laqueos auceps decideratque suos.
Intrat amor mentes usu, dediscitur usu:
   qui poterit sanum fingere, sanus erit.
Dixerit ut venias: pacta tibi nocte venito;   **505**

swirling in heat—feeling torrid, volcanic—
nevertheless, toward her,

come across colder than ice.

Act like you're totally fine. Play it cool. And
should something really bother you, don't let
her see. Laugh when you're ready to cry.* Act
like you are what you aren't and pretend the in-
sane crush is over. That's how you'll actually
make something you're trying to *fake*.

Often, to get out of drinking, I've wanted to
look like I'm sleeping, and, while I looked it,
I've felt sleep overcoming my eyes. I've had a
laugh at the chump who initially faked a love
interest—idiot!—only to get caught in his very
own trap. Love gets inside us by habit; by
habit, we learn to get past it. Those who can act
like they're fine, actually *will* become fine.

Say she's agreed to a date; then go over the
night that she promised. Say, when you get

---

* Nobody's saying you have to shut down in the heat of a moment;
such an inhuman command wouldn't comport with my plan.

veneris, et fuerit ianua clausa: feres.
Nec dic blanditias nec fac convicia posti,
    nec latus in duro limine pone tuum.
Postera lux aderit: careant tua verba querelis,
    et nulla in vultu signa dolentis habe.   510
Iam ponet fastus, quom te languere videbit;
    (hoc etiam nostra munus ab Arte feres).

Te quoque falle tamen, nec sit tibi finis amandi
    propositus: frenis saepe repugnat equus.
Utilitas lateat; quod non profitebere, fiet: 515
    quae nimis apparent retia, vitat avis.
Nec sibi tam placeat nec te contemnere possit:
    sume animos, animis cedat ut illa tuis.
¿Ianua forte patet? Quamvis revocabere, transi.

there, the door's locking you out? Suck it up.
Don't try to smooth-talk the door, and don't
flip out at it, screaming. Don't hunker down
for the night, bruising your ribs on the steps.
Come the next day, your words should all be
perfectly pleasant. Don't let the look on your
face indicate anything's wrong. Soon, she'll get
over her stuck-up self when she's sees you're
indifferent.*[35]

Still, though, you have to deceive yourself,
too. Don't set a hard deadline forcing you off
of your love; horses resist reining in. Gains
should be a surprise; what you don't make a
show of, will happen. Birds, as a rule, go around
blindingly obvious traps.

Don't let her think she's all that great, or make
you a doormat. Show some pride, and some
strength; that way, she'll see you're the boss.

Door's wide open? She's calling you in?
Too bad—keep on walking.

* This one is also a tip gleaned from my book of how-tos!

¿Est data nox? Dubita nocte venire data.   **520**

Posse pati facile est, ubi, si patientia desit,
    protinus ex facili gaudia ferre licet.

¿Et quisquam praecepta potest mea dura vocare?
    En, etiam partes conciliantis ago.
Nam quoniam variant animi, variabimus
      artes;   **525**
    mille mali species, mille salutis erunt.
Corpora vix ferro quaedam sanantur acuto;
    auxilium multis sucus et herba fuit.
¿Mollior es, neque abire potes, vinctusque
      teneris,
    et tua saevus Amor sub pede colla premit? **530**
Desine luctari; referant tua carbasa venti,
    quaque vocant flatus [*Hockings 2022:*
      fluctus *Kenney*], hac tibi remus eat.
Explenda est sitis ista tibi, qua perditus ardes;

Said she'll go out for a date? Be noncom-
    mittal that night.

Mental toughness is easy whenever—if toughness should fail—it's easy to just go have fun
(meaning, with some easy girl).

Can anyone call my prescriptions "hard"?
Can they really? Well, then just watch as I now
take the *enabler*'s role! See, because tempera-
ments vary, so too must I vary my treatments:
infinite types of disease; infinite must be the
cures. Some people's bodies do not respond to
surgical cutting; syrups and drugging alone
work to bring many relief.
    Are you weak-willed? Can't make yourself
leave? Do you feel like a captive? Cruel Love's
holding you down, pinning your neck under-
foot? Give up the struggle. Just let the winds
carry your sails—no resistance—and, by the
path the waves call, that's where to let your oars
go. Thirst is "consuming" you? "Burning" you
up? You "must" satisfy it? Fine. I get it, I do.

cedimus; e medio iam licet amne bibas.

Sed bibe plus etiam quam quod praecordia
    poscunt,   535
  gutture fac pleno sumpta redundet aqua.
I, fruere usque tua, nullo prohibente, puella;
  illa tibi noctes auferat, illa dies.
Taedia quaere mali: faciunt et taedia finem.
  iam quoque, quom credes posse carere,
    mane,   540
dum bene te cumules et copia tollat amorem,
  et fastidita non iuvet esse domo.

Fit quoque longus amor, quem diffidentia nutrit:
  hunc tu si quaeres ponere, pone metum.

Qui timet ut sua sit, ne quis sibi detrahat
    illam,   545
  ille Machaonia vix ope sanus erit.
Plus amat e natis mater plerumque duobus,
  pro cuius reditu, quod gerit arma, timet.

Go have a drink—in midstream.

Be sure to drink, though, of course, even more than your stomach requires. Water should come spilling out, gurgling up from your throat! Go on—keep at it—enjoy your girl, without interruption. Let her take all of your nights. Let her take all of your days. Aim to get sick of your illness; that "sickness" is how you will end it. Even once you're okay calling it quits, stick around. Gorge yourself—on and on—till availability kills off love, and it isn't fun being inside of that . . . house.

Also, love tends to linger when insecurity keeps it going. To get over love, ergo,

get over your fear.

Someone's afraid that his girl isn't his, that another will steal her? That man is beyond any help medical doctors can give. (Generally speaking, a mother of two will favor the son whose combat deployment, she fears, means he may never come back.)

Est prope Collinam templum venerabile
    portam;
  imposuit templo nomina celsus Eryx: 550
Est illic Lethaeus Amor, qui pectora sanat,
  inque suas gelidam lampadas addit aquam.
Illic et iuvenes votis oblivia poscunt,
  et siqua est duro capta puella viro.
Is mihi sic dixit (dubito verusne Cupido,   555
  an somnus fuerit; sed puto, somnus erat)
"O qui sollicitos modo das, modo demis
    amores,
  adice praeceptis hoc quoque, Naso, tuis.

Ad mala quisque animum referat sua, ponet
    amorem;
  omnibus illa deus plusve minusve dedit.   560

Qui Puteal Ianumque timet celeresque
    Kalendas,

Out near the Colline Gate there's a venerable
temple of Venus: "Venus of Eryx"—a name
owed to the mountain on high.[36] There's where
"Dark" Cupid dwells; He's the Cupid who
heals broken hearts, and douses, in waters of
ice, all of the flames of His torch.[37] That's
where young men come and pray, in hopes of
forgetting hopes; so do girls, when they feel
drawn to—or stuck with—a jerk. Here's what
He told me (though I'm not sure if it really was
Cupid, or just a dream in my sleep—probably
a dream, I would guess . . .):

> You—who both give people insecure love,
> and by turns, you suppress it—add to those
> maxims of yours, Ovid, this following one:

> *Everyone ought to focus*
> *on problems they have.*

> They'll forget love. God assigns problems
> to all people, to different degrees:

> Someone's anxious about making next
> month's minimum payment? Let him

torqueat hunc aeris mutua summa sui;
Cui durus pater est, ut voto cetera cedant,
   huic pater ante oculos durus habendus erit.
Hic male dotata pauper cum coniuge vivit: **565**
   uxorem fato credat obesse suo.
¿Est tibi rure bono generosae fertilis uvae
   vinea? Ne nascens usta sit uva, time.
Ille habet in reditu navem: mare semper
     iniquum
   cogitet et damno litora foeda suo.   **570**
Filius hunc miles, te filia nubilis angat;
   ¿et quis non causas mille doloris habet?
Ut posses odisse tuam, Pari, funera fratrum
   debueras oculis substituisse tuis."

remember his loans, add them all up—
and freak out.
Someone's dad is a jerk, though everything
else is just awesome? That guy should
fixate on how much of a jerk his dad is.
Someone's poor, and he lives with a wife
whose inheritance is modest? Let him
believe that his wife stands in the way of
his dreams.
Own a fine country estate that produces
excellent wine grapes? Ask yourself:
*what if the grapes shrivel and die on the
vine?*
Someone's invested in shipping? Then
ponder the hazardous sea waves—
shifting, unfair—and the coast littered
with prior attempts.
Other concerns? A son in the army . . .
your beautiful daughter. . . .

Plus, doesn't *everyone* nurse thousands of
sources of hurt? Say Prince Paris needed a
reason to make him hate Helen. Well, then,

Plura loquebatur; placidum puerilis imago   575
    destituit somnum, si modo somnus erat.

¿Quid faciam? Media navem Palinurus in unda
    deserit; ignotas cogor inire vias.

Quisquis amas, loca sola nocent: ¡loca sola
        caveto!
        ¿Quo fugis? In populo tutior esse potes.   580
Non tibi secretis (augent secreta furores)
    est opus; auxilio turba futura tibi est.
Tristis eris, si solus eris, dominaeque relictae
    ante oculos facies stabit, ut ipsa, tuos.
(Tristior idcirco nox est quam tempora
        Phoebi;   585
    quae relevet luctus, turba sodalis abest.)
Nec fuge colloquium, nec sit tibi ianua clausa,

he could recall forty-eight brothers snuffed
out. . . . [38]

That angelic form was still speaking, but all of a
sudden, *poof!* went the dream in my sleep. (If it
was only a dream.)

Well . . . what now? My captain's abandoning
ship in midocean, leaving me forced to explore
waters uncharted before. . . .

Lover, whoever you are,

avoid solitude.

Solitude is harmful. Don't withdraw; being
around people is safer for you. You don't want
places to hide—hiding places promote
paranoia—all by yourself; no, a crowd's better
protection for you. You'll get depressed if you
stay all alone; and the girl you broke up with's
face will appear in your thoughts, haunting, and
vividly real.* Don't avoid conversations. Don't

---

* That's why depression increases at night and is worse than in day-
time: none of your friends are around keeping you company then.

nec tenebris vultus flebilis abde tuos.
Semper habe Pyladen aliquem, qui curet
    Oresten:
    hīc quoque amicitiae non levis usus erit.   590

¿Quid nisi secretae laeserunt Phyllida silvae?
    certa necis causa est: incomitata fuit.
Ibat, ut Edono referens trieterica Baccho
    ire solet fusis barbara turba comis,
Et modo, qua poterat, longum spectabat in
    aequor,   595
    nunc in harenosa lassa iacebat humo.
"Perfide Demophoon!" surdas clamabat ad
    undas,
    ruptaque singultu verba loquentis erant.

Limes erat tenuis, longa subnubilus umbra,
    quo tulit illa suos ad mare saepe pedes.   600
Nona terebatur miserae via: "¡viderit!"
    inquit,
    et spectat zonam pallida facta suam,
Aspicit et ramos; dubitat, refugitque quod
    audet

shut people out, all reclusive. Don't keep your teary-eyed face hidden away in the dark. Always keep some sidekick around who can back up the hero. (Backup is a big reason why friendship is a valuable thing.)

What led to Phyllis's coming undone? The desolate forest. Left all alone as she was, that was the cause of her death: going around like a freaky trance-dancer worshipping Bacchus under a voodoo guise, tossing her hair to the wind, sometimes staring into space, looking out at the water, other times down on the ground listless, fatigued, at the shore. "Demophoon, you sonofabitch . . . !" she'd scream at the deaf waves, sobs interrupting her words, breaking them up as she spoke.

There was a narrow trail that was bridled by lengthening shadows. By it, she'd make her way out, time and again, to the sea. Time number nine that she wended her way in distress, she said, "Screw it. This is on him."

She turns pale white, and she looks at her belt. *Branches!* She sees those, too; she's not sure; she's recoiling in horror, frightened; she's

et timet, et digitos ad sua colla refert.
¡Sithoni! Tum certe vellem non sola fuisses: **605**
    non flesset positis Phyllida silva comis.
Phyllidis exemplo nimium secreta timete,
    laese vir a domina, laesa puella viro.

Praestiterat iuvenis quicquid mea Musa
        iubebat,
    inque suae portu paene salutis erat.   **610**
Reccidit, ut cupidos inter devenit amantes,
    et, quae condiderat, tela resumpsit Amor.

Siquis amas, nec vis, ¡facito contagia vites!
    Haec etiam pecori saepe nocere solent.
Dum spectant laesos oculi, laeduntur et ipsi, **615**
    multaque corporibus transitione nocent.
In loca nonnumquam siccis arentia glaebis
    de prope currenti flumine manat aqua:

touching her throat, wrapping her fingers around. . . .

Did, o Sithonian lady, you have to be all on your own then? Solitude made all the trees mourn Phyllis, shedding their leaves.

All you men hurt by a girl! All you girls hurt by a man! Phyllis should serve as your model:

Beware of excessive seclusion!

One young patient took all my advice without fail. He was on the road to recovery; he'd virtually made it to shore. But—he relapsed; he'd gotten mixed up with compulsive romantics; and, once again, Love gripped shafts decommissioned and stored.

If you're in love and you'd rather you weren't, then maintain a safe distance. Even in animals, close contact will spread a disease. Looking at addicts infects the eyes; it's addictive, infectious, and, since communicable, physical illness results. Every so often, to ground that's parched—its mud cracked to pieces—, water will gradually seep in from a river nearby.

Manat amor tectus, si non ab amante recedas,
    turbaque in hoc omnes ingeniosa sumus. **620**

Alter item iam sanus erat; vicinia laesit:
    occursum dominae non tulit ille suae.
Vulnus in antiquum rediit male firma cicatrix,
    successumque artes non habuere meae.
Proximus a tectis ignis defenditur aegre: **625**
    utile, finitimis abstinuisse locis.
Nec, quae ferre solet spatiantem porticus
       illam,
    te ferat, officium neve colatur idem.
¿Quid iuvat admonitu tepidam recalescere
       mentem?
    Alter, si possis, orbis habendus erit.   **630**

Non facile esuriens posita retinebere mensa,
    et multam saliens incitat unda sitim.

Love will seep in, unnoticed, unless you

unfriend all romantics.

(Humans: we're all predisposed *not* to find ways to do that!)

Likewise, a patient was back to being himself—but the neighborhood did him in. Bumping into his ex caused him to just . . . fall apart. Scars that hadn't healed fully, reopened; all of the old wounds came right back, and my cures didn't have any effect.

Keeping (old) flames from reaching a house next door isn't easy; safer is to just not be anywhere close to the place. Don't hang out where she shops when she's out walking. Don't try to keep up the same circles of contacts you'd had. How does reviving old memories help, once emotions are dormant?

Live, if you can, in a new—separate
and opposite—world.

Holding back is hard when you're hungry and food's on the table. Fountains of water bring

Non facile est taurum visa retinere iuvenca;
    fortis equus visae semper adhinnit equae.

Haec ubi praestiteris, ut tandem litora
        tangas,   635
    non ipsam satis est deseruisse tibi.
Et soror et mater valeant et conscia nutrix,
    et quisquis dominae pars erit ulla tuae.

Nec veniat servus, nec flens ancillula fictum
    suppliciter dominae nomine dicat "¡ave!" 640

Nec si scire voles quid agat, tamen, illa, rogabis;
    ¡Perfer! Erit lucro lingua retenta tuo.

Tu quoque, qui causam finiti reddis amoris,
    deque tua domina multa querenda refers,
Parce queri; melius sic ulciscere tacendo,   645

on terrible feelings of thirst. Holding back a bull is hard when it's spotted a heifer. Stallions nicker, without fail, when they've spotted a mare.

Finally—after you've done all that—to reach terra firma, it won't do just to cut ties with your ex herself.

Part ways, too, with her mother, her sister,
her chaperone/confidante, and with any
and all others who are part of her life.

So, no letting a servant come by. No letting her lady's maid, with her crocodile tears, whisper, "My mistress says 'hi.'"
    What if you're wondering how she is? Forget it—just don't ask. Patience! Hang on! You'll find holding your tongue is for the best.

Furthermore, if you're explaining why the relationship ended—citing a litany of outrages, blaming your ex—,

don't air your grievances.

ut desideriis effluat illa tuis.
Et malim taceas quam te desisse loquaris:
   qui nimium multis "non amo" dicit, amat.

Sed meliore fide paulatim extinguitur ignis
   quam subito: lente desine, tutus eris.   **650**
Flumine perpetuo torrens solet altior ire:
   sed tamen haec brevis est, illa perennis
      aqua.
Fallat, et in tenues evanidus exeat auras,
   perque gradus molles emoriatur amor.

Sed modo dilectam scelus est odisse
      puellam;   **655**
   exitus ingeniis convenit iste feris.
Non curare sat est: odio qui finit amorem,
   aut amat, aut aegre desinet esse miser.
Turpe vir et mulier, iuncti modo, protinus hostes;
   non illas lites Appias ipsa probat.   **660**
Saepe reas faciunt, et amant; ubi nulla
      simultas

Silence is better for getting revenge, since that way, you'll get her flushed out of your system and thoughts. Also, I'd rather that you say nothing than claim that you're past it. If you keep saying, "I don't love her" to people, it's a good sign you still do.

Putting the fire out little by little's more promising, though, than snuffing it out all at once. Slowly pull back; you'll be safe. Typically, yes, flash floods rise higher than regular rivers; still, they don't last very long. Rivers, though, never run out. Let love quietly fade and evaporate into the ether, and, by gentle degrees, gradually dwindle and die.

Still, it's perverse to *hate* your ex—the woman you just cared for! Hating your ex in the end? That's something psychopaths do! Being indifferent is plenty; a person whose love ends in hatred either enjoys, or at least struggles to quit, feeling bad. Two people going from partners to enemies? All in an instant? Awful. Even divorce lawyers don't want to see that.

Often, men sue their ex—but still love them.

incidit, admonitu liber aberrat Amor.

Forte aderam iuveni; dominam lectica tenebat:
    horrebant saevis omnia verba minis.
Iamque vadaturus "lectica prodeat" inquit;   **665**
    prodierat: visa coniuge mutus erat.
Et manus et manibus duplices cecidere
      tabellae,
    venit in amplexus, atque ita "vincis" ait.
Tutius est aptumque magis discedere pace,
    nec petere a thalamis litigiosa fora.   **670**
Munera quae dederas, habeat sine lite, iubeto:
    esse solent magno damna minora bono.
Quod si vos aliquis casus conducet in unum,
    mente memor tota, quae damus, arma tene.

Nunc opus est armis; hīc, o fortissime,
    ¡pugna!   **675**

*Absent a lawsuit, Love wanders off some-
where else, free from His need to appear.*

Once, I was with a young client; his wife was
waiting nearby, out in the carriage. Every word
out of his mouth crackled with furious threats.
Set on divorce right there, he exclaimed, "Get
her out of that carriage!" So, she got out, and he
fell—silent: he'd *looked* at his wife. Both his
hands dropped; as they did, they were dropping
divorce papers with them. Over he went for a
hug, saying, "You win." (That's the end.)

Splitting up is safer—more dignified, too—
when it's amicable, see, rather than leaving the
sheets only to go lawyer up. As for the gifts that
you gave her? She keeps 'em. Tell her. No lawyers.
Littler losses like those tend to do good in the end.

But, if events somehow conspire to bring you
together: then, and with all of your heart—

stick to your guns

—as I've taught. *Now* you need weapons!
This is the moment! *Fight*, you tough soldier!

vincenda est telo Penthesilea tuo.
Nunc tibi rivalis, nunc durum limen amanti,
  nunc subeant mediis irrita verba deis.

Nec compone comas, quia sis venturus ad
    illam,
  nec toga sit laxo conspicienda sinu.   680
Nulla sit, ut placeas alienae cura puellae;
  iam facito e multis una sit illa tibi.

Sed quid praecipue nostris conatibus obstet
  eloquar, exemplo quemque docente suo.
Desinimus tarde, quia nos speramus amari: 685
  dum sibi quisque placet, credula turba sumus.
At tu nec voces (¿quid enim fallacius illis?)
  crede nec aeternos pondus habere deos.

Penthesilea must fall—brought to the ground by your spear.[39] *Now* let the memories come flooding back: the rival, the shut door deaf to your calling, the lies—told in clear sight of the gods . . . !

Don't bother combing your hair just because you are going to see her.

Don't wear your toga all loose, draped in the latest style. Don't give the slightest regard to impressing somebody else's girlfriend. Do what you must, so for you, she's just a face in the crowd.

Let me reveal the main obstacle hampering all of our efforts. I'll give the template, so see how your experience fits: *We're all slow to break up because we assume that she loves us.* All of us like ourselves, so we're the credulous type.

Don't be.

Refuse to believe her sweet nothings.

What's more deceptive? Anything? And refuse to believe that *"I swear, by the gods!"* means anything in her oaths.

Neve puellarum lacrimis moveare, caveto:
    ut flerent, oculos erudiere suos.   **690**
Artibus innumeris mens oppugnatur amantum,
    ut lapis aequoreis undique pulsus aquis.
Nec causas aperi quare divortia malis,
    nec dic quid doleas; clam tamen usque dole.
Nec peccata refer, ne diluat: ipse favebis,   **695**
    ut melior causa causa sit illa tua.

Qui silet, est firmus; qui dicit multa puellae
    probra, satisfieri postulat ille sibi.

Non ego Dulichio furari more sagittas,
    nec raptas ausim tinguere in amne faces;   **700**
Nec nos purpureas pueri resecabimus alas,
    nec sacer arte mea laxior arcus erit.
Consilium est, quodcumque cano: parete
    canenti,

*Be on guard against letting the tears of
an ex unnerve you.*

They train their eyes so they can weep on de-
mand. Infinite tricks of the trade undermine
your resolve when you're smitten, much as a
rock out at sea is constantly battered by waves.
Don't disclose the reasons why breaking up is
your preference. Don't say why you're aggrieved. (Inwardly, though, hold a grudge.)
Don't list her sins: she'd only explain them
away, and you'll end up helping make her case
seem more justified than your own.

Silence is strength.

A person who's always angrily accusing his ex
indicates he needs reassurance from her.
   Unlike Ulysses, I wouldn't dare misappro-
priate arrows; no grabbing torches, and no putting them out in a stream.[40] I won't be clipping
the glimmering wings of a little boy, either, or
sabotaging His bow. Those aren't the tricks of my
trade. Counseling is all that my poem is providing,

tuque favens [*as in Henderson:* utque facis
　　Kenney] coeptis, Phoebe saluber, ades.
Phoebus adest: sonuere lyrae, sonuere
　　pharetrae;   705
　　signa deum nosco per sua: Phoebus adest.

Confer Amyclaeis medicatum vellus aenis
　　murice cum Tyrio; turpius illud erit.
Vos quoque formosis vestras conferte puellas;
　　incipiet dominae quemque pudere suae;   710
utraque formosae Paridi potuere videri,
　　sed sibi conlatam vicit utramque Venus.

Nec solam faciem, mores quoque confer et artes:
　　tantùm iudicio ne tuus obsit amor.

Exiguum est quod deinde canam,
　　sed profuit illud   715
　　exiguum multis, in quibus ipse fui.

so trust your provider. And, lord Apollo—I
pray—come bless our efforts with health.
              [*sounds are heard*]
    Listen! Apollo is here! Those sounds: His
lyre! His quiver! Those are His signs, I can tell!
Yes, it's Apollo, He's *here!*

Take and put fleece that's chemically treated in
dye vats in Sparta next to purple from Tyre; it'll
be shoddier stuff. Each of you, too, should

> *compare your girlfriend with*
> *ravishing women.*

Look at your lady, and soon, each of you *will*
feel ashamed. Though in the judgment of Paris,
Minerva and Juno were beauties, Venus compared each to Herself: looked at together, She won.
    Not just her face, though; also compare per-
sonalities, skill sets. (Just don't let love impair,
though, any judgment of yours.)
    What I'll say next is small but important. It's
helped a great many, small though it is—and
among them, I'm including myself.

Scripta cave relegas blandae servata puellae:
   constantes animos scripta relecta movent.
Omnia pone feros (pones invitus) in ignes,
   et dic "ardoris sit rogus iste mei."   720
Thestias absentem succendit stipite natum:
   ¿tu timide flammae perfida verba dabis?

Si potes, et ceras remove: ¿quid imagine muta
   carperis? Hoc periit Laodamia modo.

Et loca saepe nocent; fugito loca conscia
     vestri   725
   Concubitus; causas illa doloris habent.
"Hīc fuit, hīc cubuit; thalamo dormivimus illo:
   hīc mihi lasciva gaudia nocte dedit."

*Don't reread old texts that you got, and
you saved, from your girlfriend.*

Rereading texts from an ex softens the stoniest
heart. Put all those messages—no, you won't want
to—into a roaring fire, and say, "May this serve
as the pyre of my love." Thestias burned (via
brand, in his absence) her son (Meleager). You'll,
though, hesitate to give lying words to the flames?[41]
    If you can swing it,

get rid of her pictures.

Why are you stuck on phantoms? That's what
cost Laodamia her life.[42]
    Places can be problematic, too.

*Avoid places that witnessed encounters
the two of you had.*

Those trigger feelings of grief: "Here's where
she lived . . . and here's where she'd eat . . . that's
the bedroom we slept in . . . here, one adventur-
ous night, we had incredible sex."

Admonitu refricatur amor, vulnusque novatum
    scinditur: infirmis culpa pusilla nocet.   730
Ut, paene extinctum cinerem si sulphure
      tangas,
   vivet et e minimo maximus ignis erit,
sic, nisi vitâris quidquid renovabit amorem,
    flamma redardescet, quae modo nulla fuit.
Argolides cuperent fugisse Capherea
      puppes,   735
   teque, senex, luctus ignibus ulte tuos.
Praeterita cautus Niseide navita gaudet:
    tu loca, quae nimium grata fuere, cave.
Haec tibi sint Syrtes, haec Acroceraunia ¡vita!
    Hīc vomit epotas dira Charybdis aquas.   740

Sunt quae non possunt aliquo cogente iuberi,
    saepe tamen casu facta levare solent.
Perdat opes Phaedra, parces, Neptune, nepoti,

Love recrudesces when chafed by reminders; they rub till the wound splits open all over
again. Tiny mistakes harm the weak. Just as
when embers are all but extinguished: you
touch 'em with sulfur, fire comes roaring to life,
going from nothing to huge—, so, unless you
avoid those things that'll bring love to life,
love's flame will flare up anew, though it was totally out. Greeks going home from Troy would
have done better evading Caphereus and the revenge a bereaved father exacted with fires.[43]

Painstaking sailors rejoice the moment they
make it past Scylla. *You* must take pains to evade
places you loved in the past. Treat them like
danger zones to steer clear of, like shallows or
rock reefs. That's where Charybdis barfs up all
the liquid she's chugged.[44]

Try as we might, there are some situations
we simply can't order into existence, but when
chance makes them happen, they help:

Phaedra, say, grows up poor? Well, Neptune, You'll spare her stepson, since his

nec faciet pavidos taurus avitus equos.
Cnosida fecisses inopem, sapienter amasset: 745
   divitiis alitur luxuriosus amor.
¿Cur nemo est, Hecalen, nulla est, quae ceperit
    Iron?
   Nempe quod alter egens, altera pauper erat.

Non habet, unde suum paupertas pascat
    amorem;
   non tamen hoc tanti est, pauper ut esse
    velis.   750

At tanti tibi sit non indulgere theatris,
   dum bene de vacuo pectore cedat amor.
Enervant animos citharae lotosque lyraeque
   et vox et numeris bracchia mota suis.
Illic assidue ficti saltantur amantes: 755

grandaddy's bull won't get to panic his
   steeds.[45]
Picture Pasiphae and Ariadne as paupers.
   They'd both be smart about love, since
   wealth stimulates decadent love.[46]
Why would no man go after Hecale? No
   woman Irus? Obviously, it's because
   one was a beggar, one poor.

Poverty lacks the resources to feed and
sustain a relationship

. . . though that's not good enough reason to
want to be poor!
   It would be smart, that said, to

abstain from theatrical stage shows

until love can recede, leaving your head good
and clear. Feelings grow sappy and soft at the
citharas, auloses, lyres, voices, and arms in the
air rhythmically matching the songs. Stereo-
typically lovesick guys are *always* on stage

†quid caveas actor qua iuvet arte docet.†

Eloquar invitus: ¡teneros ne tange poetas!
   summoveo dotes impius ipse meas.
Callimachum fugito, non est inimicus Amori;
   et cum Callimacho, tu quoque,
      Coe, noces.   760
Me certe Sappho meliorem fecit amicae,
   nec rigidos mores Teia Musa dedit.
¿Carmina quis potuit tutò legisse Tibulli,
   vel tua, cuius opus Cynthia sola fuit?
¿Quis poterit lecto durus discedere—Gallo? 765
   Et mea nescioquid carmina tale sonant.

there, and, in those roles, they enact scenes to avoid—if you can.

This one hurts, but I'll say it:

Hands off the erotica poets. *

You shall run from Callimachus; he has no
  problem with Cupid.
Likewise, Philétas of Cos does (like Cal-
  limachus) harm.
Sappho assuredly upped my own game
  with a girlfriend.
The "muse from Teos" (Anacreon)
  preached, "Old inhibitions, begone!"
Who could read through the poems of
  Tibullus and manage to hold out?
Or of Propertius, for whom Cynthia filled
  every page?
Who will be able to get out of bed feeling
  hard, after reading Gallus?
(*Ahem*) My own poems hit some similar
  notes. . . .

---

* Yes, I am banning my own—sacrilege!—gifts to the world.

Quod nisi dux operis vatem frustratur Apollo,
    aemulus est nostri maxima causa mali.
At tu rivalem noli tibi fingere quemquam,
    inque suo solam crede iacere toro.   770

Acrius Hermionen ideo dilexit Orestes,
    esse quod alterius coeperat illa viri.
¿Quid, Menelae, doles? Ibas sine coniuge
        Creten,
    et poteras nupta lentus abesse tua.
Ut Paris hanc rapuit, nunc demum uxore
      carere   775
    non potes: alterius crevit amore tuus.

Hoc et in abducta Briseide flebat Achilles,
    illam Plisthenio gaudia ferre viro.
Nec frustra flebat, mihi credite: fecit Atrides,
    quod si non faceret, turpiter esset iners.   780
Certe ego fecissem, nec sum sapientior illo:

But—if our guru Apollo's not fooling His prophet, then—it's her new boyfriend who's the main cause underlying our woes. You, though, shouldn't convince yourself that you're in competition with some guy. No, instead:

Imagine she's sleeping alone.

What drove Hermione's lover, Orestes, to want her so badly? Well, because some other man started to have her himself.[47]

What's Menelaus complaining about? He went off to Crete without Helen and seemed fine being away from his bride. Now that Paris has nabbed her, he feels like he can't do without his wife. It's because his love grew from another man's love.

That's why Achilles was rankled: Briseis got stolen, then started pleasuring Pleisthenes's son—lord Agamemnon—in bed. (Oh, and he wasn't rankled for nothing. Trust me, the warlord would've been one sad chump not to behave as he did. I would have done it myself,

invidiae fructus maximus ille fuit.
Nam sibi quod numquam tactam Briseida iurat
   per sceptrum, sceptrum non putat esse deos.

Di faciant, possis dominae transire relictae   **785**
   limina, proposito sufficiantque pedes.
Et poteris, modo velle ¡tene! nunc fortiter ire,
   nunc opus est celeri subdere calcar equo.
Illo Lotophagos, illo Sirenas in antro
   esse puta; remis adice vela tuis.   **790**

Hunc quoque, quo quondam nimium rivale
      dolebas,
   vellem desineres hostis habere loco.
At certe, quamvis odio remanente, saluta;
   oscula quom poteris iam dare, sanus eris.

and I am no wiser than he was, since, of that whole sorry mess, sex was the ultimate prize. To the extent Agamemnon swore by his scepter he'd never touched Briseis, he thought, "Scepters? They aren't the gods!"[48])

May the gods grant you the strength to pass by the door of the girl you broke up with. May they make your feet able and up to the task.[49] And—you *can!* You can *do* it! Hang on, because *this* is the moment, *this* is the time! So be brave kicking your horse, and take off. Tell yourself: "In that cave lurk Lotus Eaters; in that cave, Sirens are waiting," and add sails to help power your oars.

   As for the man who's been constantly rankling you (your "replacement")? Now I'd like you to stop thinking of him as a foe. You may well still hate the guy, but

acknowledge his presence.

Once you can kiss his cheek, that's when you'll know that you're cured!

Ecce, cibos etiam, medicinae fungar ut omni 795
   munere, quos fugias quosque sequare,
     dabo.
Daunius, an Libycis bulbus tibi missus ab
     oris,
   an veniat Megaris, noxius omnis erit.
Nec minus erucas aptum vitare salaces,
   et quicquid Veneri corpora nostra parat. 800
Utilius sumas acuentes lumina rutas,
   et quidquid Veneri corpora nostra negat.

¿Quid tibi praecipiam de Bacchi munere,
     quaeris?
   Spe brevius, monitis expediere meis.
Vina parant animum Veneri, nisi plurima
     sumas   805
   et stupeant multo corda sepulta mero.
Nutritur vento, vento restinguitur ignis:
   lenis alit flammas, grandior aura necat.
Aut nulla ebrietas, aut tanta sit, ut tibi curas

Speaking of which, I'll append some remarks
on diet and foods to eat or avoid (to complete
our comprehensive approach):

Onions—whether Italian, or Libyan im-
ports, or coming to you from Megara—
they're dangerous, every last one.[50]
No less wise is avoiding arugula (it makes
people horny) and aphrodisiacs, which
arouse our bodies for sex.
Better for you to eat rue, which sharpens
the eyesight, as well as anaphrodisiacs,
which turn off our bodies for sex.

Curious what advice I have to give you re:
Bacchus? Here—my incredibly short recommendations for you: Wine psychologically
primes us for sex, if you don't overdo it, ending
up wasted, because alcohol has buried your
brain. Fire is nourished by wind, and by wind
is a fire extinguished. Light ventilation will coax
flames, heavy put them to death. So, then,

*don't get drunk at all, or get yourself so
drunk that you forget all your woes.*

eripiat: si qua est inter utrumque, nocet.   810

■ ■ ■

Hoc opus exegi: fessae date serta carinae;
   contigimus portus, quo mihi cursus erat.
Postmodo reddetis sacro pia vota poetae,
   carmine sanati femina virque meo.

—FINIS—

Anything less interferes.

■ ■ ■

This is the end of my work. Give me garlands to hang on my tired ship's keel! We've come into port right where I'd charted the course. Soon you'll be offering prayers of thanks, as you should, to your poet, all of you women and men healed by the words of my song.

—THE END—

OVID'S THIRTY-EIGHT REMEDIES FOR LOVE

In a perfect world, says Ovid, we'll nip a bad relationship in the bud. But we don't live in a perfect world, so failing that, we must wait for an infatuation to die down. Once it does, and we're ready for treatment, these thirty-eight tips will help us get over it.

1. *Never have "nothing to do."* In other words, keep yourself occupied at all times.
2. *Go out and fight on campaign—wearing a toga, downtown.* In plain English, become a lawyer.
3. *Heed the call of duty.* That is, join the army.
4. *Farm life can easily fix any fixation you have.* Get out of the city and back to nature, because "farmacology" beats pharmacology.

5. *Venus has often turned tail and shamefully fled after Diana prevails!* In other words, cultivate an outdoor hobby: take up hunting or fishing or bird catching.
6. *Get out and go far away. Take a long trip out of town.* Out of sight, out of mind. . . .
7. *Place not your faith in spells, abracadabras, and charms.* Spells, magic, tarot, crystals—avoid it all. It's bunkum.
8. *Fixate on all that you lost, fixate on all that she cost.* Count up all the money and emotion you invested in the relationship, and you'll feel resentment grow. Imprudent, but effective.
9. *Minimize and belittle your ex's best features.* Tell yourself your ex is nowhere near as attractive or talented as you thought, especially if it's not true. A recommendation borrowed from Lucretius.
10. *Go in the morning and drop in on her, all unannounced.* Catching your ladylove without makeup gives you an unfiltered view of reality.

11. *Go hump a random girl first.* Crass, evil, but presumably effective in the short term.
12. *Adopt an outrageous sex position—an abnormal, unflattering one.* A second reality check, also evil.
13. *Juggle a couple of partners.* Go get a new flame—a second girlfriend or boyfriend will divert your attention and your affection simultaneously.
14. *Come across colder than ice.* By acting indifferent, you'll become indifferent ("Fake it till you make it.").
15. *Go have a drink—in midstream.* Specifically, keep having sex until you're sick of it.
16. *Get over your fear.* Suppress jealousy.
17. *Everyone ought to focus on problems they have.* Anxiety kills all the joy in life.
18. *Avoid solitude.* Strength in numbers!
19. *Unfriend all romantics.* Ovid offers us the first of three case histories to argue that being around happy people in love is bad for us.

20. *Live, if you can, in a new—separate and opposite—world.* It's best in a breakup to avoid all the places your ex is likely to be. Ovid gives us a second case history to illustrate the point.

21. *Part ways with her mother, her sister, her chaperone/confidante, and with any and all others who are part of her life.* A breakup means breaking up with your ex's family, too. One of Ovid's saddest recommendations.

22. *Don't air your grievances.* Feelings will just come flooding back.

23. *Absent a lawsuit, Love wanders off somewhere else, free from His need to appear.* Litigation risks reconciliation. Our third case history.

24. *Stick to your guns.* Get tough and don't cave.

25. *Don't bother combing your hair just because you are going to see her.* More generally, don't dress to please your ex.

26. *Refuse to believe her sweet nothings.* Be deaf to entreaty.
27. *Be on guard against letting the tears of an ex unnerve you.* I'm crying, you're not crying.
28. *Silence is strength.* Forgo recrimination.
29. *Compare your girlfriend with ravishing women.* Evil, but probably effective (at least until guilt sets in).
30. *Don't reread old texts that you got, and you saved, from your girlfriend.* We have phones, the Romans had wax tablets, but the principle is the same.
31. *Get rid of her pictures.* We have Instagram, they had frescoes.
32. *Avoid places that witnessed encounters the two of you had.* Shun the haunts of your happier times.
33. *Poverty lacks the resources to feed and sustain a relationship.* You shouldn't choose poverty, but if you *are* poor, it helps.
34. *Abstain from theatrical stage shows.* No tearjerker movies for you.

35. *Hands off the erotica poets*. Erotic fiction makes it hard to concentrate.

36. *Imagine she's sleeping alone; acknowledge your rival's presence*. Stop brooding on your ex's new flame. And when you can finally greet the new partner with a kiss on the cheek, it's a dispositive sign that you're cured.

37. *Don't eat onions or arugula; do eat rue*. They're aphrodisiacs or anaphrodisiacs, respectively (says Ovid).

38. *Don't get drunk at all, or get yourself so drunk that you forget all your woes*. Tipsiness brings back all kinds of emotions. (In the sixteenth century, the poet Vincent Obsopoeus made this one recommendation the basis for his sequel to Ovid's poem, *How to Drink*.)

Ovidius nimium amator ingenii sui, laudandus
tamen partibus.
Ovid was too in love with his own wit, but
    parts of his work merit praise all the same.
—QUINTILIAN (C. 100 CE), *THE EDUCATION*
    OF THE ORATOR 10.89

. . . Nuper enim nostros quidam carpsere
    libellos,
  quorum censura Musa proterva mea est.
Dummodo sic placeam, dum toto canter in orbe,
  qui volet, impugnent unus et alter opus.
Ingenium magni livor detractat Homeri;   **365**
  quisquis es, ex illo, Zoile, nomen habes.
Et tua sacrilegae laniarunt carmina linguae,

THE ARTIST'S MANIFESTO

Between lines 360 and 399, Ovid inserts a digression to defend his art against charges of obscenity. The defense is a braggadocious manifesto; it insists that because all artistic genres require certain kinds of content, Ovid's own chosen genre, elegy, requires frisky subject matter. The digression is important but distracting, so for this edition I've relocated it here.

. . . Recently, see, some people took issue with books that I've published. These censorious souls say that my music's "obscene."

Well, while I'm winning applause—while my praises are ringing out worldwide—fine. Let a critic or two carp at my work if they want! Envious slander maligns the genius of Homer— our greatest! Every last "zoilus" is named for that first one of all.[51] Blasphemous cynics have even savaged the poems of Virgil—*Virgil!*—

pertulit huc victos, quo duce, Troia deos.
Summa petit livor; perflant altissima venti;
   summa petunt dextra fulmina missa Iovis. 370
At tu, quicumque es, quem nostra licentia
     laedit,
   si sapis, ad numeros exige quidque suos.
Fortia Maeonio gaudent pede bella referri;
   deliciis illic ¿quis locus esse potest?
Grande sonant tragici: tragicos decet ira
     cothurnos; 375
   usibus e mediis soccus habendus erit.
Liber in adversos hostes stringatur iambus,
   seu celer, extremum seu trahat ille pedem.
Blanda pharetratos Elegia cantet Amores,
   et levis arbitrio ludat amica suo. 380
Callimachi numeris non est dicendus
     Achilles,
   Cydippe non est oris, Homere, tui.
¿Quis ferat Andromaches peragentem Thaida
     partes?
   Peccet, in Andromache Thaida quisquis agat.
Thais in arte mea est; lascivia libera
     nostra est; 385

whose leadership saw Troy bring her gods here to Rome.[52] Envy targets the tops. Winds bluster and howl at the summits. Lightning targets the tops, fired by Jupiter's hand.

Look, whoever you are that's upset at my freewheeling spirit: Think!—if you can—and take *poetry* into account. Legends of war enjoy being sung in the meter of Homer. How could heroic verse domicile sexcapades there? Tragedy's tone is stately; wrath belongs in its raiments, whereas for sitcom scenes, comfortable flip-flops are right. Freedom of speech needs iambs unholstered to fight back an army— strafing consistently, or misfiring every sixth round.[53] Elegy's silky strains should sing of romantic relationships: she's a flirty girl(friend); so, let her flirt as she likes.[54]

So, Achilles does not belong in the meter I'm using, and Cydippe's all wrong, Homer, for your epic verse.[55] No one would tolerate Thais playing the part of Andromache; Andromache played Thais-like would be absurd.[56] Thais is what my art *does*; my approach is freewheeling,

nil mihi cum vitta; Thais in arte mea est.
Si mea materiae respondet Musa iocosae,
   vicimus, et falsi criminis acta rea est.
¡Rumpere, Livor edax! Magnum iam nomen
    habemus;
   maius erit, tantùm quo pede coepit eat.   390
Sed nimium properas: vivam modo, plura
    dolebis;
   et capiunt animi carmina multa mei.
Nam iuvat et studium famae mihi crevit honore;
   principio clivi noster anhelat equus.
Tantum se nobis elegi debere fatentur,   395
   quantum Vergilio nobile debet epos.
Hactenus invidiae respondimus: attrahe lora
   fortius, et gyro curre, poeta, tuo.

sexy! "Good" girls aren't my thing; Thais is what my art does. Hence, if my poetry answers the call of its friskier subject matter, case closed—for my Muse clearly was falsely accused.

Bite me, you envious haters, Ovid's *already* found stardom! I'll be a superstar, too—if I keep doing my thing.

Oh, and you're getting ahead of yourselves. If I live, you'll regret it more: I have *lots* of poems knocking around in my head. See, I like getting famous—and am, like I'm getting respected. My time is now; this ride's raring to take off and go. Elegy artists owe me as much— they admit it themselves—as lordly epic owes Virgil for all its success.

Basta! We've answered the haters enough. Now pull it together, artist, and rein yourself in. Time to get back on the track.

ABOUT THIS EDITION

The Latin text is that of E. J. Kenney 1994, though I've repunctuated it, changed the conjunction *cum* to *quom*, and preferred a different reading here or there. With Kenney, I omit lines 25–26 and 405–6 as spurious and I mark line 756 as corrupt beyond repair. Following some manuscripts, I've also set the first few words of lines 79 and 399 in small capital letters to mark the two major divisions of the treatise.

NOTES

1. Holmes and Rahe 1967.
2. The fragments of Antiphon's works are found in Laks and Most 2016. The block quotations are fragments P10 + P9, *Getting Along* is *On Concord* D41–D63, and *The Interpretation of Dreams* is P1c + D75–D77. "Antidepressant" translates *nepenthe*, the drug administered by Circe in Homer's *Odyssey*; like any good huckster, Antiphon meant the name ironically.
3. *Tristia* 4.10.
4. Henderson 1979, xii: "The *Remedia* may therefore have been published (i.e., out of Ovid's hands) as early as the third, or even the second, quarter of A.D. 1, supposing that he had more or less completed it when he heard of Gaius' advance." Less specific estimates say 1 BCE–2 CE. (The sole criterion for dating the poem is the reference to Gaius Caesar's military advance in lines 155–58.)

5. 3.34.81–82; tr. Curtius 2021. An influential example was a book titled *Therapies* by the Stoic philosopher Chrysippus. Chrysippus's book is lost, but traces of it survive in *How to Keep Your Cool* and *How to Grieve*.

6. 4.35.73–75; tr. Curtius 2021.

7. *Commentary on Hippocrates' Epidemics*, tr. Wack 1990, 8. Galen's best-known account of "diagnosing" (that is, detecting) lovesickness is found in chapter 6 of *On Prognosis*.

8. "Amor qui et eros dicitur morbus est cerebro contiguus" (*Viaticum* 1.20; Wack 1990, 186). Wack 1990, 3–50 is a masterful reconstruction of the history.

9. Bianchi Bensimon 2018, 183: "[T]i può chiarire Amore non solamente essere . . . ad infirmità simile, ma esser vera infirmità e periculosa."

10. Robertson and Codd III 2019.

11. The answer to these two rhetorical questions is implied by a pun: *cur aliquis* (why have some men) suggests *cura* (girlfriend). The translation "Why have" (pronounced *why've*), implying "wife," is meant to replicate this effect.

12. This is not a metaphor. In ancient Greece and Rome, suitors would hang elaborate festoons on

the doorways of private houses to signal romantic interest (Yates 1875, with pictures).

13. Some commentators think this disclaimer was inserted later, because it doesn't entirely ring true with what follows. But perhaps Ovid does mean what he says, and his advice does work both ways.

14. Ovid now reminds his readers of disastrous love affairs in Greek (or for Dido, Roman) mythology—stories he expects you to either know or go look up. He'll come back to Phyllis and her story in line 591. The unnamed third heroine is Medea, next mentioned in 261.

15. This Scylla is the princess of Megara and daughter of Nisus, not the sea monster who lives in the Straits of Messina.

16. The longer you put off facing up to reality, says Ovid, the harder it will be. Twenty years earlier, Ovid's older contemporary Horace had expressed the same idea differently: *Dimidium facti qui coepit habet: sapere aude!* ("He who has begun is half done, so be bold! Wise up!") In time, the last two words became the unofficial motto of the Enlightenment.

17. In mythology, Myrrha seduced her father and was subsequently changed into a myrrh tree.
18. That is, keep having sex without getting attached. (As the addict says, "I can quit anytime.")
19. A legendary archer, Philoctetes suffered a disgusting illness caused by a wound and was abandoned on the island of Lemnos. Eventually called back into service, he helped the Greeks win the Trojan War.
20. According to ancient lore (e.g., Pliny *Natural History* 12.8), wine was poured at the base of plane trees to stimulate growth. The average reader in ancient Rome would no more have known this than you or I; Ovid is simply showing off a factoid he picked up somewhere.
21. The Parthians (Iranians) were *not* the Romans' next triumph, which is one reason scholars can date our work so precisely (see note 4). By "speaking of which" Ovid means both (1) soldiering, and (2) retreat, for which the Parthians were proverbially famous. In combat, Parthian soldiers would retreat on horseback while firing arrows back at their enemy. The name of this tactic, known as a "Parthian shot," was later

corrupted in English to a "parting shot." Ovid here connects the Parthians' proverbial moniker with, apparently, a contemporary bona fide retreat of their army before the forces of Gaius Caesar.

22. When Agamemnon went off to fight the Trojan War, Aegisthus—the original "Jody" of military legend—moved in and seduced ("got busy" with) his wife. Since Aegisthus was from Mycenae, "Argos" here must mean simply "Greece." Ovid surely chose it because *Árgos* sounds like *argós*, "idle, having nothing to do."

23. Diana (Greek Artemis) is goddess of the hunt and, for some, the patron goddess of Men Going Their Own Way (see Euripides's tragedy *Hippolytus* and note 45).

24. Like 9/11 in the USA, "Allia" denoted a day of national trauma in ancient Rome. Originally the name of a nearby river, it became shorthand for a disastrous conflict in 387 BCE that saw Gallic invaders defeat Rome on the battlefield and then sack the city.

25. A region of northern Greece, Thessaly was the Transylvania of ancient Rome: a spooky realm of sorcery and witchcraft.

26. Medea and her aunt, Circe, are antiquity's two most famous witches. Medea was the classic, orientalized Other from the dark lands of Georgia (on the Black Sea); she was used and abused by the Greek hero Jason, who eventually abandoned her for another woman. Circe is discussed in the Quick Start Guide.

27. Podalirius was a Greek medical officer at Troy. To Roman ears, his name suggested *delirium* (madness, infatuation).

28. Phineus was tormented by Harpies, nasty birds with women's faces who would swoop in and poop all over his food every time he tried to eat it.

29. No, the translation is not mistaken. Ovid's examples do not make the point he says they will, but rather the opposite point. Interpret the blunder how you will.

30. Another litany of rare mythological names whose stories Ovid doesn't really expect you to know (or go look up), since the point he's making is clear.

31. Since Chryses's meddling is about to set the *Iliad* in motion, Ovid upbraids him directly. We're meant to envision the scene that begins in *Iliad* 1.1.

32. Briseis.

33. Love/cured/lovesickness: Ovid makes a highly wrought pun on two meanings of Latin *cura* (lovesickness; girlfriend) and Greek *koúre* (maiden), which is Homer's preferred word for both Briseis and Chryseis. In other words, one *koúre* (maiden) "cures" *cura* (lovesickness).

34. Ovid is plugging books 1 and 3 of *The Art of Love*, which explain exactly where in the city of Rome available men and women can find each other.

35. The reference is to Ovid's *The Art of Love* 1.715–718.

36. Mt. Eryx in Sicily, where an ancient temple to Astarte (Venus, Aphrodite) stood.

37. Dark (or "Darth") Cupid is Ovid's invention, and seems to be the first example of the "evil counterpart" or "evil clone" motif in Western literature. His powers are the reverse of the real Cupid: whereas Real Cupid (*verus Cupido*) makes it impossible to forget someone, this infernal, nightmare version has the power to make the lovelorn *forget* the object of their love.

38. In the Trojan War. Only a single brother, Helenus, survived the Trojan War, which was caused by Paris's romance or rape of Helen.

39. Penthesilea was an elite Amazon warrior in the Trojan War. She slew many Greek soldiers until she was slain in turn by Achilles.
40. Ulysses "stole" Philoctetes's arrows by manipulating him into rejoining the Trojan War (see note 19).
41. "Thestias" means Althaea, daughter of Thestius. When Meleager killed her brothers, she burned a magic log that had been preserving his life. (She then died by suicide.)
42. When her husband, Protesilaus, was killed in the Trojan War, Laodamia had a bronze image of him made. Her father soon caught her fetishizing the image; he destroyed it, and she took her life in grief.
43. Angry at their fatal abuse of his son Palamedes, Nauplius would shine false lights from Caphereus (a promontory on the coast of Argos) to lure homebound Greek ships to their doom.
44. Ovid imagines Charybdis, the whirlpool in Homer's *Odyssey*, as a binge drinker who's had too much and is now regurgitating all kinds of things better kept down—like memories.
45. Phaedra falsely accused Hippolytus of rape. His credulous father, Theseus, implored his own

father, the god Neptune, to destroy Hippolytus. Neptune did so by causing a bull to appear, spook Hippolytus's horses, and cause a fatal crash.

46. Ovid's allusion in Latin to "the woman of Cnossus" is ambiguous. It could mean either Pasiphae, the queen of Cnossus who fell in love with a bull (but not the bull of the preceding line), or princess Ariadne (who fell in love with Theseus, husband of Phaedra in the previous line, and then ran off with him before being abandoned by him). My translation splits the difference.

47. The "other man" was Neoptolemus, son of Achilles. Hermione had been betrothed to Orestes, but her father rebetrothed her to Neoptolemus—whom Orestes eventually killed.

48. Ovid misremembers (possibly on purpose) *Iliad* 1.233–39, where Achilles—not Agamemnon—swears by Agamemnon's scepter. In fact, Agamemnon *did* swear by the gods that he hadn't slept with Briseis (*Iliad* 19.258–65).

49. This couplet, which deals with addiction to a person, bears a striking resemblance to the "Serenity Prayer" used in Alcoholics Anonymous

and other twelve-step recovery programs: "God grant me the serenity to accept the things I cannot change, the courage to change the things I can, and the wisdom to know the difference." Since the modern prayer is ultimately indebted to the Stoic Epictetus, it may well be that Ovid is parodying some Stoic mutual aid organization of his own time.

50. Technically not "onions" but hyacinth bulbs, called *lampascioni* in Italian and *volví* in Greek.

51. A "zoilus" is "a bitter and usually enviously carping critic; one given to unjust quibbling and fault-finding" (Merriam-Webster). The noun comes from the first Zoilus, a notorious fourth-century BCE critic of Homer's *Iliad* and *Odyssey*.

52. The allusion is to Virgil's *Aeneid*.

53. Iambic verse, which is used for invective, came in two varieties: the "pure" iambic trimeter and the "limping" variety, the latter of which unexpectedly "drags" out every sixth foot.

54. "Elegy" is the meter Ovid uses for love poetry (see the introduction).

55. Achilles is the epic hero of the *Iliad*. Cydippe, a legendary maiden of Athens, was tricked into marrying Acontius. A poem about their affair,

now lost, was written in elegiac couplets by the famous poet Callimachus. Ovid gives his own version in *Heroides* 20 and 21 (also in elegiac couplets).

56. Andromache is the legendary widow of Hector, greatest of the Trojan heroes. Thais was a real courtesan of fourth-century Athens who had, like Marilyn Monroe, passed into legend herself. Her name eventually became a byword for a glamorous, unabashed, and hypersexualized woman.

BIBLIOGRAPHY

Henderson's 1979 commentary is excellent on all aspects of the poem, and warmly recommended.

Bianchi Bensimon, Nella, ed. 2018. *Battista Fregoso: Anteros*. Milan: Leonard Pachel.

Curtius, Quintus, tr. 2021. *Cicero: Tusculan Disputations*. Fortress of the Mind.

Henderson, A.A.R., ed. 1979. *Ovid: Remedia Amoris*. Edinburgh: Scottish Academic Press.

Hockings, T.A.J. 2022. "Conjectures on Ovid's Love Poems." *Acta Classica* 65:65–94.

Holmes, Thomas H., and Richard H. Rahe. 1967. "The Social Readjustment Rating Scale." *Journal of Psychosomatic Research* 11:213–18.

Kenney, E. J., ed. 1994. *P. Ovidi Nasonis Amores; Medicamina Faciei Femineae; Ars Amatoria; Remedia Amoris*. 2nd ed. Oxford: Clarendon.

Laks, André, and Glenn W. Most, eds. 2016. *Early Greek Philosophy.* Vol. 9, *Sophists, pt. 2*. (Loeb). Boston: Harvard University Press.

Robertson, Donald, and Trent Codd III. 2019. "Stoic Philosophy as a Cognitive Behavioral Therapy." *The Behavior Therapist* 42:42–50.

Wack, Mary Frances. 1990. *Lovesickness in the Middle Ages*. Philadelphia: University of Pennsylvania Press.

Yates, James. 1875. "Serta." In *A Dictionary of Greek and Roman Antiquities*, edited by William Smith, pp. 1029–30. London: John Murray. Online at https://tinyurl.com/sertae.